the art & design series

For beginners, students, and professionals in both fine and commercial arts, these books offer practical how-to introductions to a variety of areas in contemporary art and design.

Each illustrated volume is written by a working artist, a specialist in his or her field, and each concentrates on an individual area—from advertising layout or printmaking to interior design, painting, and cartooning, among others. Each contains information that artists will find useful in the studio, in the classroom, and in the marketplace.

Some of the books in the series:

Chinese Painting in Four Seasons: A Manual of Aesthetics & Techniques, Leslie Tseng-Tseng Yu / text with Gail Schiller Tuchman

Display Design: An Introduction to Window Display, Point-of-Purchase, Signs and Signages, Sales Environments, and Exhibit Displays, Laszlo Roth

Drawing: The Creative Process, Seymour Simmons III and Marc S.A. Winer

Drawing with Pastels, Ron Lister

Graphic Illustration: Tools & Techniques for Beginning Illustrators, Marta Thoma

An Introduction to Design: Basic Ideas and Applications for Paintings or the Printed Page, Robin Landa

The Language of Layout, Bud Donahue

Painting and Drawing: Discovering Your Own Visual Language, Anthony Toney

Portrait Drawing: A Practical Guide for Today's Artists, Lois McArdle

A Practical Guide for Beginning Painters, Thomas Griffith

Transparent Watercolor: Painting Methods and Materials, Inessa Derkatsch

Understanding Paintings: The Elements of Composition, Frederick Malins

elizabeth resnick

GRAPHIC DESIGN

A PROBLEM-SOLVING APPROACH TO VISUAL COMMUNICATION

Prentice-Hall, Inc., Englewood Cliffs, New Jersey 07632

Library of Congress Cataloging in Publication Data

Resnick, Elizabeth.
  Graphic design.

  (The Art & design series)
  "A Spectrum Book".
  Bibliography: p.
  Includes index.
  1. Printing, Practical.   2. Graphic arts.   I. Title.
II. Series.
Z253.R39   1984   686.2'24   83-13981
ISBN 0-13-363267-9
ISBN 0-13-363259-8 (pbk.)

This book is available at a special discount when ordered in bulk quantities. Contact Prentice-Hall, Inc., General Publishing Division, Special Sales, Englewood Cliffs, N.J. 07632.

The Art & Design Series

© 1984 by Prentice-Hall, Inc., Englewood Cliffs, New Jersey 07632

A SPECTRUM BOOK

ISBN 0-13-363267-9

ISBN 0-13-363259-8 {PBK.}

All rights reserved. No part of this book may be reproduced in any form or by any means without permission in writing from the publisher.

10 9 8 7 6 5 4 3 2 1

Printed in the United States of America

Editorial/production supervision by Maria Carella
Cover design by Hal Siegel
Manufacturing buyers: Christine Johnston
and Edward J. Ellis

Prentice-Hall International, Inc., *London*
Prentice-Hall of Australia Pty. Limited, *Sydney*
Prentice-Hall Canada Inc., *Toronto*
Prentice-Hall of India Private Limited, *New Delhi*
Prentice-Hall of Japan, Inc., *Tokyo*
Prentice-Hall of Southeast Asia Pte. Ltd., *Singapore*
Whitehall Books Limited, *Wellington, New Zealand*
Editora Prentice-Hall do Brasil Ltda., *Rio de Janeiro*

I am truly appreciative of the talented students who so generously contributed materials for illustration and those friends and colleagues who had encouraging words for this project.

A special thank you to Malcolm Grear of the Rhode Island School of Design for his inspiring concept of design education; to Paul Rand for his thoughts on design; to Gary Davis for preparing the illustrations in the section on materials; to The Massachusetts College of Art and Al Gowan; to Mary E. Kennan, my editor, for her encouragement and support of this book project; and a personal thank you to Maria Carella, my production editor, for her excellent job of editing the manuscript.

Elizabeth Resnick, a freelance graphic designer, is an assistant professor of design at The Massachusetts College of Art in Boston.

To Herb Lubalin, Ivan Chermayeff, and Hermann Zapf, whose excellent work has always inspired me;

to all my wonderfully creative students at The Massachusetts College of Art, for teaching me about teaching;

to my parents, Sylvia and Seymour Resnick, for the many years and countless ways they have encouraged my artwork;

to my husband, Victor Cockburn, for his patient and loving support during the time it took to prepare this manuscript;

and to our son, Alexei, the next generation of creative potential...

this book is dedicated.

contents

Foreword   ix

INTRODUCTION   1

one / THE LETTERFORM COLLAGE   9

two / THE RELATIONSHIP OF LETTERS   23

three / LETTERFORM PROGRESSIONS   37

four / WORD ACTION PROGRESSION   51

five / WORD PLAY TYPOGRAPHY   61

six / SELF-PROMOTION TYPOGRAPHY   71

seven / THE SIMPLE TOOL   81

eight / THE QUOTE POSTER   91

nine / THE VEGETABLE POSTER   103

ten / THE COUNTRY POSTER   125

Bibliography   143

Index   147

foreword

There have been few books in my nearly twenty years as a design educator that I could recommend to design students. The books published have been terribly dated, hopelessly slanted toward tools and materials, or merely pretty gazettes of award-winning designs without a clue as to how those solutions were reached.

The art education of most students does not prepare them for a career in graphic design. Most art education centers on personal expression and nonjudgmental evaluation. In art this is a correct assumption, but for young designers trying to communicate in a clear, unambiguous way with an audience they will never see, it is hardly adequate. Basic notions of composition, color, line, and "art" are less important than *what* is shown. The process of how to get a message across—using your client's money, not your own—must be repeatable or you will not be a graphic designer very long.

On rare occasions personal expression and effectiveness merge, but given a choice, the responsible designer must choose effectiveness. In her book Elizabeth Resnick is giving us her process of how this can be done. She states the objectives of a class problem, assigns it before our eyes, lists references and materials, and gives us a tough assessment of the solutions.

If her book is successful, design teachers will find their students creating design messages that may be more effective than this book's illustrations. Nobody would be happier than Elizabeth Resnick if this happens, for she will be trying in her own classes to do the same thing—refining a process that will allow a student to come up with not one but several excellent designs.

Al Gowan
Chairman, Design Department
The Massachusetts College of Art

INTRODUCTION

INTRODUCTION

Graphic design is visual communication design with an emphasis on conveying information with meaning and significance. In their work graphic designers employ typography, illustration, symbolism, and photography, often in various combinations, to communicate ideas in visual terms.

The role of the graphic designer in today's society is evolving. Principally concerned with layout and production in past decades, the graphic designer is now becoming involved with more socially responsible communication. This implies the designer's awareness of what is said *and* how to say it effectively for maximum outreach.

Primary education must be concerned with design as a fundamental discipline. Learning and understanding concepts and principles of visual communication are essential components of visual literacy or the personal goal of a professional design practice. The development of a design vocabulary and a philosophy of problem-solving methodologies is the springboard that stimulates your imagination to innovate rather than imitate. Design educators cannot "create" designers, but they can help students become sensitive to design by encouraging them to develop their own innate creative potential. Teaching basic tools and principles through design progressions initiates creative mental processes instead of fostering solutions of a purely cosmetic nature.

The structure of this book is intended to make teaching and learning more effective. Each chapter proposes one specific visual exercise designed for you to analyze and interpret. Success in these assignments is the result of determination, careful thought, and plain hard work. The evidence of what has already been accomplished by past students stands as a good benchmark, indicating what *can* be achieved. Yet, this material is only a beginning for the serious student of design.

INTRODUCTION

You must continue to seek out further sources of ideas and instruction to build upon this foundation.

Aimed primarily at first-year design students, this book can be used for all levels, from secondary school students to those taking advanced courses to those practicing designers interested in expanding their creative potential.

ON MATERIALS

The current art supplies market abounds with good-quality materials available through local art store outlets and mail order catalogs.

Choosing your materials wisely is very important, since their cost is forever skyrocketing in our modern economy. The investment in good-quality materials will, from the very beginning, save you money. If you buy poor-quality materials (usually because they are inexpensive at the time of purchase), you will need to replace them frequently at current market prices. Good working tools assist greatly in the creation of good design, saving you from frustration and wasted time.

The following is a very basic list of tools and materials you will need during the course of solving each of the ten problems stated in this book. The necessary materials can be purchased as needed. An additional list of materials follows each of the assignment descriptions.

1. *T-square* (figure 1): Wood and acrylic T-squares damage too easily, although they are inexpensive. I suggest a lightweight aluminum T-square, which is perfect for ruling and cutting.

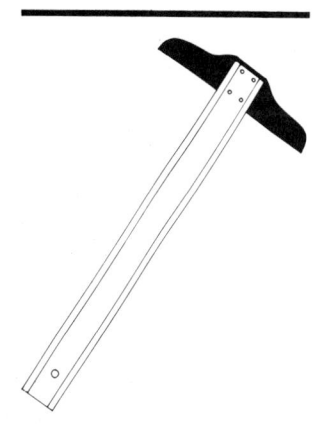

1 T-square

The drawings of materials here and on the next few pages are by Gary Davis.

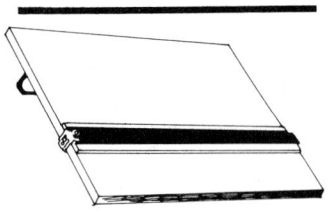

INTRODUCTION

2. *Parallel-rule drawing board* (figure 2; optional equipment): This is a metal-edged drawing board with a parallel-rule attachment and plastic-tipped elevators for use on desk or table top. The parallel rule would replace the need to purchase a T-square.

3. *18" or 24" metal ruler:* These rulers are used for ruling and cutting.

4. *Triangles* (30°/60°/90° and 45°; figure 3): These plastic or aluminum triangles are used for ruling and cutting. Aluminum triangles fare better for cutting; plastic can be nicked, which ruins the straight-edge for ruling.

5. *Compass and ruling pen set* (figures 4 and 5): Combination bow compass with interchangeable ruling pen and pencil attachment for ruling in ink and designers gouache.

6. *Technical fountain pen* (figure 6): These pens (also called rapidographs) are used for drawing and ruling. There are many brands of technical pens and any person trying them will come to choose a favorite after using a few different types. All technical pens do need care to keep them running smoothly. They will clog up if they are not used regularly and should be cleaned out periodically. You should have at least two or three different points: #00, #1, and #2 are standard equipment.

7. *Black India ink and black technical fountain pen ink* (figure 7): Black India ink is very opaque and waterproof. It is good for filling in large black areas with a brush. India ink can be used in a ruling pen but should not be used in a technical fountain pen. You will need an ink labeled for technical pens.

8. *Brushes* (figure 8): The most important part of a brush is the hair. The highest grade of hair is known as red sable. Other grades are less expensive and tend to "shed" their hairs. You will need

2 Parallel-rule drawing board

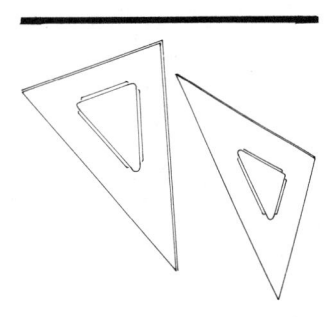

3 Triangles

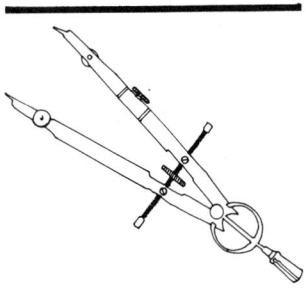

4 Compass with interchangeable ruling pen attachment

5 Ruling pen

INTRODUCTION

several sizes of brush: #00, #1, and #3 are good choices.

9. *Pencils:* You will need hard leads for drafting; 2H and 3H are fine. Regular yellow pencils are good for sketching.

10. *Erasers* (figure 9): There are several different types of eraser for various uses. You will need a kneaded rubber eraser for erasing soft pencil lines and smudges; a gum eraser for heavier lines and general cleanup; and a plastic eraser for removal of ink lines and other materials.

11. *X-acto® knife and extra blades* (figure 10): The standard #11 X-acto® knife is fine for cutting paper surfaces. A pack of extra blades is necessary, since the blade edges dull quickly.

12. *Utility knife* (also called mat knife; figure 11): This knife is used for scoring and cutting of thick surfaces. The blade should be retractable into the knife handle for safety in storage.

13. *Rubber cement* (figure 12): A quality adhesive like 2-coat Best-Test® Rubber Cement provides good adhesion yet can be removed easily without leaving a trace. You can buy this cement in a small can with a brush or in quart and gallon containers.

14. *Rubber cement solvent and dispenser* (figure 13): This solvent is necessary for thinning thickened rubber cement. It comes in a valvespout dispenser for removing rubber cement-mounted material.

15. *Rubber cement pick-up* (figure 14): A small square of crepe rubber made for the removal of excess rubber cement from around edges and on surfaces.

16. *Masking tape and drafting tape:* Masking tape is used for bonding two pieces of board together and for more permanent adhesion of any surface to another. Drafting tape is used to hold

6 Technical fountain pen

7 Black ink

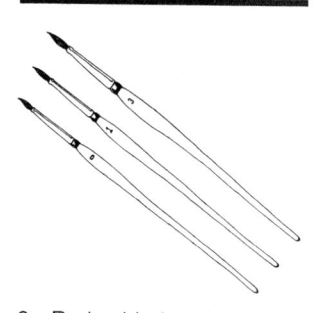

8 Red sable brushes

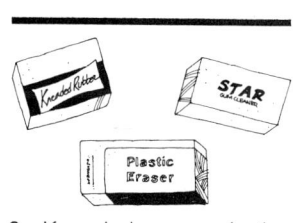

9 Kneaded eraser, plastic eraser, gum eraser

INTRODUCTION

10 #11 X-acto® knife and extra blades

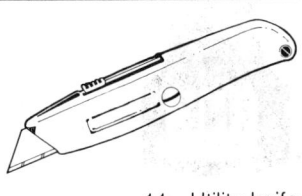

11 Utility knife

12 Can of rubber cement

material in place while working, and will not pull up the edges of your paper or board.

17. *Tracing paper in pad or roll:* A transparent paper used for preliminary sketching and working out visual solutions. I find the roll of inexpensive white or yellow tracing paper to be the most economical, as you can cut the required amount of paper for each sketch.

18. *Color-Aid paper:* This paper has a silkscreen-coated surface with a matte finish. It is available at art supply stores in 220 coordinated colors and is used for the finishes on cut-paper assignments.

19. *Pantone® Color Paper:* Pantone® paper has a printed color surface available at art supply stores in five hundred colors. It, too, is used for the finishes on cut-paper assignments.

20. *Designers gouache:* A water-based paint with an exceptionally smooth flow and good opacity and covering power.

21. *Illustration board, Bainbridge No. 172:* A fine quality board with a smooth surface. It is especially good for black ink work and for many other design purposes.

22. *Type book:* You will need a good, up-to-date book of typeface specimens. I always advise my students to collect prestype catalogs like the Letraset Catalog, as they always contain the most current typefaces available and are either free or very inexpensive. They are available through most art supply stores or through the mail from distributors. Other recommended sources for good type specimens are:

Gates, David. *Type.* Watson-Guptill, 1973.

INTRODUCTION

International Typeface Corporation type specimen booklets available through *U&lc, The International Journal of Typographics*, 2 Hammarskjold Plaza, New York, N.Y. 10017.

Longyear, William. *Type and Lettering.* Watson-Guptill, 1966.

Rosen, Ben. *Type and Typography.* Van Nostrand Reinhold, 1963.

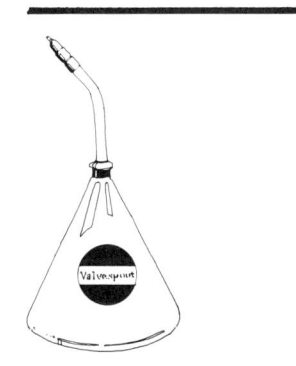

13 Rubber cement solvent dispenser

MAIL ORDER ART SUPPLIES

Good quality professional art supplies are available by mail order through catalogues produced annually by the following companies:

A.I. Friedman, Inc.
37 West 53 Street
New York, New York 10019

A.J. Ardons
176 Brookline Avenue
Boston, Massachusetts 02215

14 Rubber cement pick-up

Alvin & Co., Inc.
Box 188
Winsor, Connecticut 06095

Alvin & Co., Inc.
Box 1975
San Leandro, California 94577

Charrette Corporation
31 Olympia Avenue
Woburn, Massachusetts 01801

INTRODUCTION

Charrette Corporation
212 East 54 Street
New York, New York 10022

Dick Blick
Box 1267
Galesburg, Illinois 61401

Flax Art Supplies
4554 North Central Avenue
Phoenix, Arizona 85012

Flax Art Supplies
10852 Lindbrook Drive
Los Angeles, California 90024

Flax Art Supplies
250 Sutter Street
San Francisco, California 94108

Martin Instrument Company
13450 Farmington Road
Livonia, Michigan 48150

New York Central Supply
62 Third Avenue
New York, New York 10003

Sam Flax
1515 Spring Street NW
Atlanta, Georgia 30309

Sam Flax
55 East 55 Street
New York, New York 10022

Sam Flax
2606 Oaklawn Avenue
Dallas, Texas 75219

one
THE LETTERFORM COLLAGE

THE LETTERFORM COLLAGE

Typography can be viewed as two-dimensional architecture on which a foundation of visual communication can be built. The individual letters, when placed one next to the other in a predetermined plan, form the building blocks in creating a thought or idea.

Typography as a communication medium can take many directions and acquire as many forms. In order to understand the building components of any graphic message, we need to look at letters individually. To begin the study of graphic design, I have always felt the importance of exploring the positive and negative shapes created by letterforms rather than their language implications. Achieving good results in typographic expression lies within the careful analysis of letterforms and their individual structures.

For example, as everyone knows, the A is the beginning of our alphabet. But its identity does not stop there. The A is also a shape made up of converging lines forming a triangular shape. Looking within this triangular shape, you will notice another more solid similiar shape (figure 15). When another letter, such as a B, is placed to the right of the A, we find another shape created between the spaces of the two letterforms (figure 16). This shape is a right-angled triangle.

In addition to form, letterforms can also express movement and rhythm. Movement within and around typography is an important aspect of visual language. It can illustrate an idea or concept by use of spatial dimensions within the two-dimensional format. In analyzing what makes a composition interesting to the viewer, the student might discover the use of foreground, middle, and background elements set up to bring the viewer into the scene by the use of spatial planes. Such devices also create a movement *around* the picture

15   The letterform A with its negative shape

16   The letters A and B with the angular shape created by placing the two letters together

THE LETTERFORM COLLAGE

plane, enabling all elements to be experienced individually and as a whole entity, bringing forth the idea intended by the designer.

The straights and curves, verticals and horizontals of letters, when grouped together in certain formations, can produce a rhythmic pattern or strong directional movement (figure 17).

After considering form and movement, we can also speak of type as having texture and color. The thin and thick strokes and varying weights of letterforms create different textures. When grouped together or multiplied, the effort can show interesting patterns, textures, and colors (figure 18).

The letterform collage assignment is designed to explore letters as form and in terms of movement and texture. We begin by clipping single letters from magazines. These letters should be black and printed on a white background, or white letters printed on a black background. There should be no color or shades of grey in the letters or in the backgrounds. When you clip the letters, leave a little background surrounding each letter (figure 19). You will need to cut many different sizes and weights of letters to be prepared to begin your design. I estimate you should cut at least one hundred single letters, and perhaps more as your design progresses.

On a sheet of 8 x 10" white or black paper, place a handful of your cut-out letters in random order. Begin by moving around certain letters. Notice the individual relationships created by placing one letter next to another and then another. As you discover these spatial relationships begin to formulate an idea or direction you wish to pursue. An idea is simply a plan of action. Do you wish your design to reflect a landscape, sea waves, an endless tunnel? Once an idea takes hold, create a layout in

visual*design*visual*design*visual*design*
visual*design*visual*design*visual*design*
visual*design*visual*design*visual*design*
visual*design*visual*design*visual*design*
visual*design*visual*design*visual*design*
visual*design*visual*design*visual*design*
visual*design*visual*design*visual*design*
visual*design*visual*design*visual*design*
visual*design*visual*design*visual*design*
visual*design*visual*design*visual*design*
visual*design*visual*design*visual*design*

17 Rhythmic letterform pattern

THE LETTERFORM COLLAGE

Type*Type*Type*Type*Type*Type*Type*Type*
Type*Type*Type*Type*Type*Type*Type*Type*
Type*Type*Type*Type*Type*Type*Type*Type*
Type*Type*Type*Type*Type*Type*Type*Type*
Type*Type*Type*Type*Type*Type*Type*Type*
Type*Type*Type*Type*Type*Type*Type*Type*
Type*Type*Type*Type*Type*Type*Type*Type*
Type*Type*Type*Type*Type*Type*Type*Type*
Type*Type*Type*Type*Type*Type*Type*Type*
Type*Type*Type*Type*Type*Type*Type*Type*
Type*Type*Type*Type*Type*Type*Type*Type*
Type*Type*Type*Type*Type*Type*Type*Type*

18 Textural letterform pattern

19 Black letter surrounded by a white background

your mind. Resist the urge to pencil in any sketch lines onto the paper. Do not make the letters conform to a prearranged shape, but allow the letters to express their individual shapes when creating an area in your composition. The most successful solutions to this problem are the most spontaneous, requiring no drawn plans, only spatial arrangement solidified by an idea and by arrangement of letters according to their shape relationships. Paste each letter down individually in its designated position once your design decision is made. Upon completion mount your design centered on a 12 x 14" board.

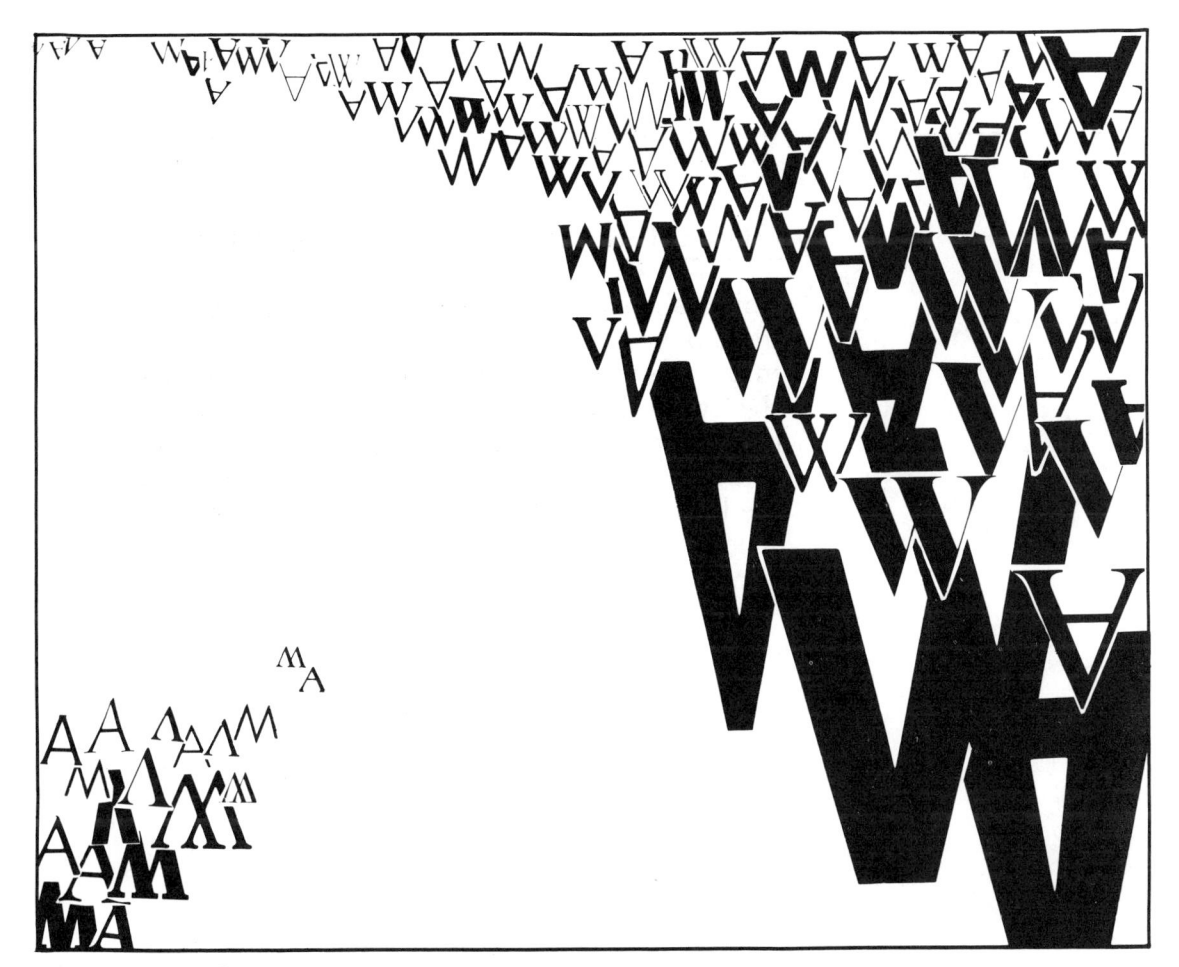

20 Kit Crowe
Each student chooses direction by stressing form, movement, or texture, although all three must be expressed to some degree in each study. The success of this study relies on the imagery of visual movement created by the letterforms. The student chose similarly shaped letterforms (A,W,V) to produce a uniform, angular direction of coming forward. The feeling of a large crowd of people surging forward with a strong sense of depth is achieved by the use of small letters in the background which gradually increase in size to the much larger letters in the foreground.

THE LETTERFORM COLLAGE ASSIGNMENT

This assignment is a study of letterforms as *form, movement,* and *texture.* Clip single letters from magazines you have around the house. Remember: the letters should be black on a white background or white on a black background, and there should be no shades of grey or color in either the letters or the backgrounds. Place these cut-out letters on a sheet of 8 x 10" white or black paper and create form, movement, and texture.

Materials needed

1. 8 x 10" white or black paper
2. Magazines
3. Scissors or #11 X-acto® knife for cutting
4. Rubber cement
5. Rubber cement solvent in a valvespout dispenser
6. Rubber cement pick-up
7. 12 x 14" sheet of mat board in white or black

Reference

Craig, James. *Designing with Type.* New York: Watson-Guptill Publications, 1971.

Dürer, Albrecht. *Of The Just Shaping of Letters.* New York: Dover Publications, 1965.

Hofmann, Armin. *Graphic Design Manual.* New York: Van Nostrand Reinhold, 1965.

Wong, Wucius. *Principles of Two-Dimensional Design.* New York: Van Nostrand Reinhold, 1972.

21 David P. White
Movement is the dominant theme in this study. The student takes full advantage of form and perspective to convey a real sense of gushing forward. He uses negative space to define and silhouette the movement, accentuating the force of the flow. Here the letterforms make up a textural quality that supports its movement.

THE LETTERFORM COLLAGE

22 Janet Palasek
The scene in this study is reminiscent of an aerial view of Times Square in New York City before the stroke of midnight bringing in the new year. I feel the student achieves a very rich, textural quality by the juxtaposition of negative and positive letterforms in varying sizes.

23 Tracy Wampler
In this study, reminiscent of mountainous forms, the textural areas infiltrate one another and in the process carve out strong white shapes.

20

THE LETTERFORM COLLAGE

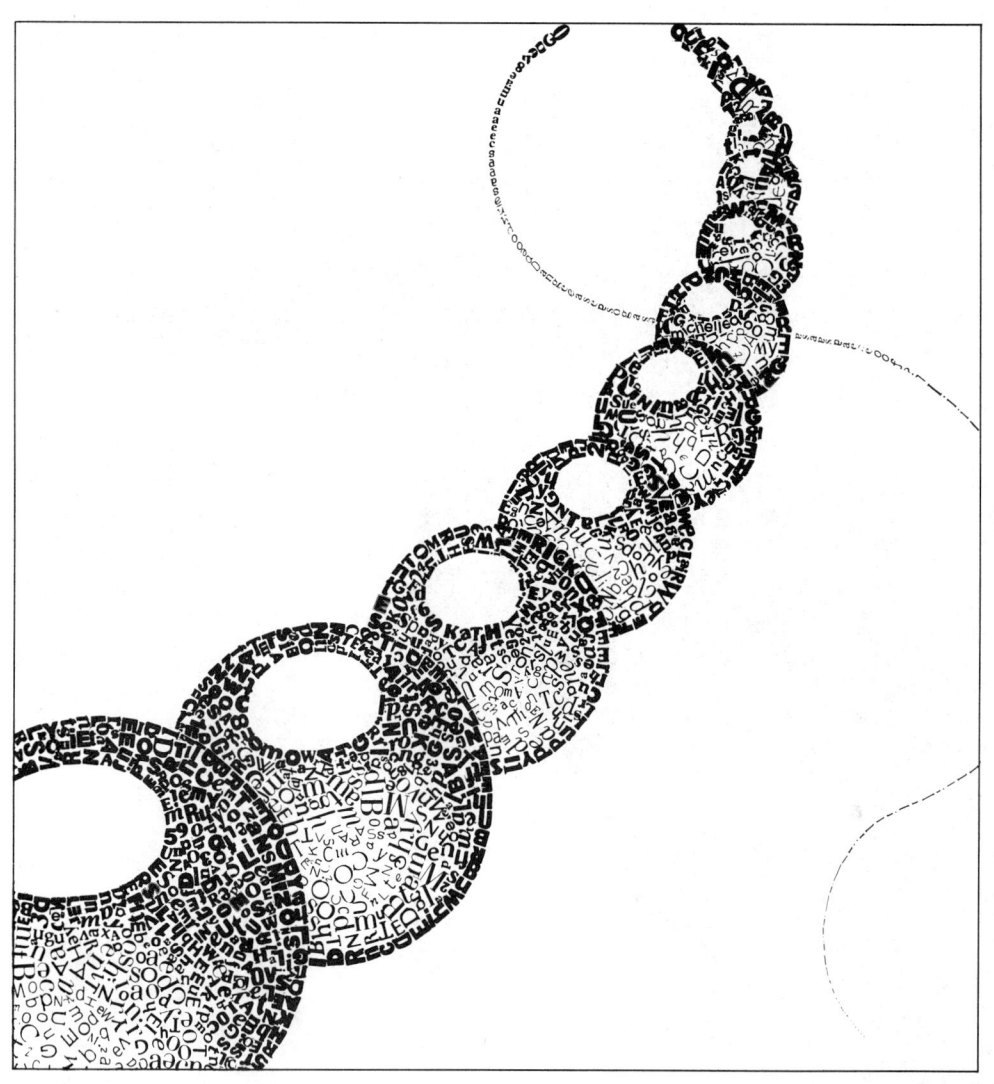

24 Dan Gee
The diagonal movement of the open-topped spheres sweep the viewer up from the lower left corner of this composition and back into a space of infinity. With the use of multi-weight letters and intricate detailing, this student creates an exciting three-dimensional illusion.

25 Judith Anthony
Texture and movement are the primary elements in this study. Clusters of letterforms surround an ever-diminishing "tunnel" we can follow to infinity. The student achieves this effect by orchestrating the black letters—they rise from the bottom of the composition, narrow, and recede into the tunnel shape. The top half of the composition is composed of white letters which form the background plane.

26 Lynne Ramirez
You can imagine the mighty force of a cyclone as it whips through well defined negative (background) shapes. I especially enjoy the rich textural quality of this study.

two
THE RELATIONSHIP OF LETTERS

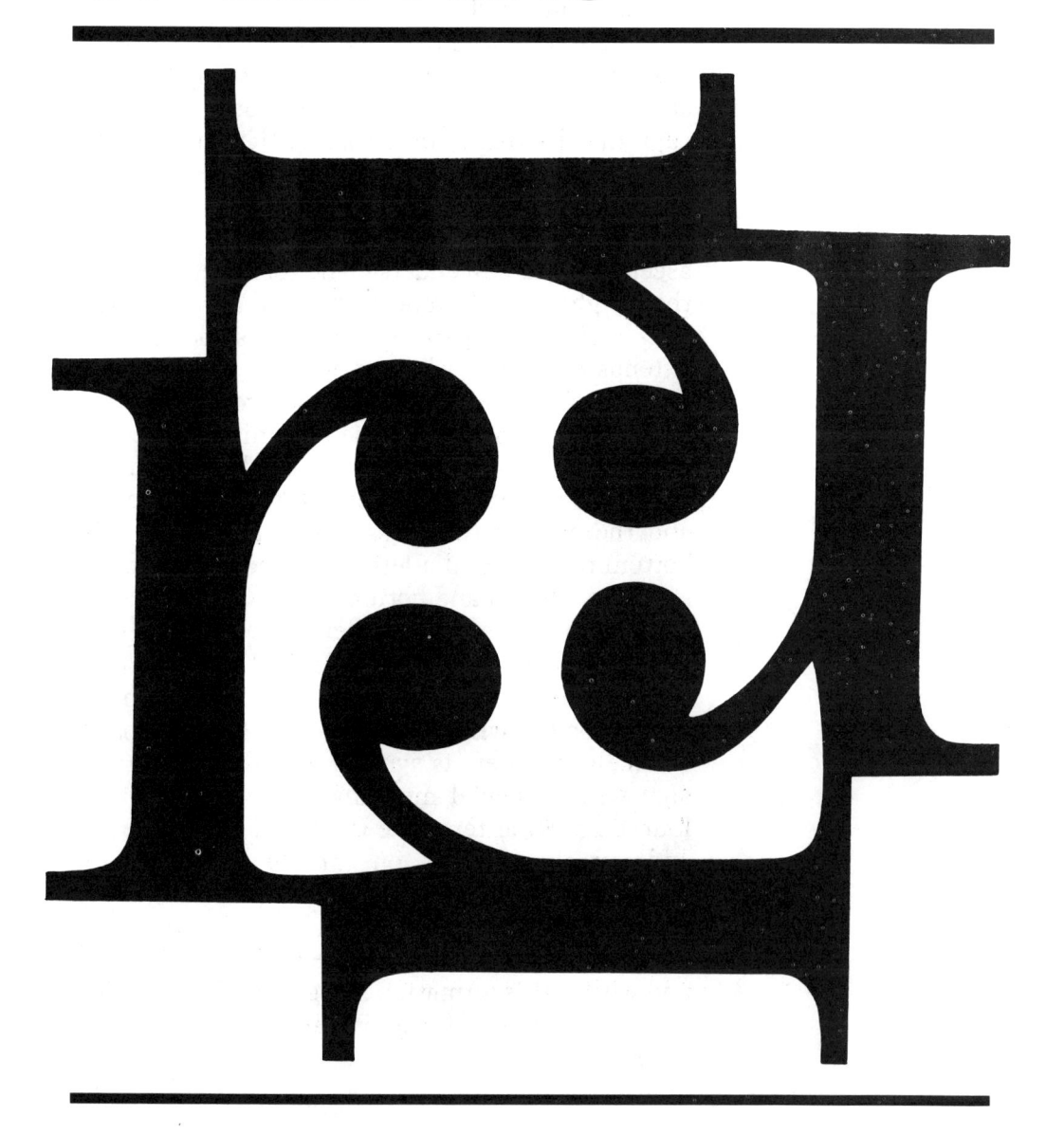

THE RELATIONSHIP OF LETTERS

In our modern world we are surrounded by typography in the form of signs, advertisements, books, magazines, and television. Typography exists wherever and whenever a visual message needs to be communicated.

It is important for the student to learn the basic language (terminology) of typography. Look at figure 27. *Uppercase* is a term used to denote capitalized letters. *Lowercase* is the term for the small letters. *X-height* is the measurement for the height of the main element of a lowercase letter (that is, the height of the lowercase letter without ascenders and descenders). The term derives from the height of a lowercase "x" in any typeface. *Ascender* is the part of a lowercase letter that extends above the x-height, and the *descender* is the part of a lowercase letter that drops below the *baseline,* the common plane on which the letters are placed. A *counter* is the enclosed space within a letter. The *stem* is the vertical stroke of a letter, and the *serif* is the cross stroke at the top and bottom of a letter. If a letter does not have a cross stroke at the top and bottom, it is said to be *sans serif* (without a serif—see figure 28).

A letterform can be defined as a symbol representing a sound used in speech, or as any of the symbols of which written words are composed. The key word here is *symbol,* which is a mark or sign with a special meaning. If we were to take four identical letters, like the four Fs in figure 29, and put them facing one another in a certain configuration, we would achieve something more than just four letters. We would discover a unique symbol composed of a positive figure (the four Fs) and within this formation a negative figure formed by a combination of negative areas from the original four Fs.

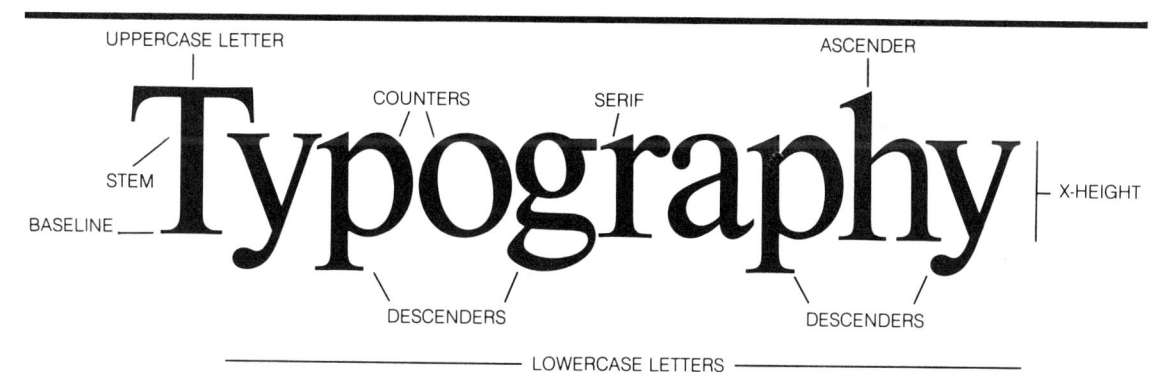

27 The terminology of typography

28 Sans serif typography

29 F configuration

As we continue our exploration of the positive and negative image areas existing in and around letterforms, we can't help but notice that a configuration like figure 29 could be viewed as an exercise in discovering one method to be used in the design of a typographic symbol or subsequent trademark.

In addition to this exercise serving as an invaluable tool in beginning the thought process of developing a typographic symbol, it teaches the student to look beyond the positive shape aspects of a form to its inner shape qualities and the shapes created by its natural boundaries. The materials needed to begin this study are simple: tracing paper, pencil, and a typebook or prestype catalogue. The first letter of your last name is your assigned letterform. (I always assign a letter because I have found that too much time is spent in search of the ideal alphabetic letter to use.) It is best to start off this assignment with one letter in mind, taking it through all the necessary explorations required to go beyond the first simple solutions. The more complex arrangements (although ultimately quite simple in nature) come about after all the obvious first thoughts and sketches have been exhausted.

Begin by choosing a particular typeface, such as Garamond, Helvetica, or Palatino. Trace your assigned letter on your sheet of tracing paper and follow in suit by tracing three more like the first in a symmetrical order. The letterforms cannot overlap but they can touch one another. (They do not *need* to be put in a symmetrical order, although it does help in creating a stronger negative-image area.) After trying about twenty different configurations with the same typeface, continue with other typefaces, using both serif and

THE RELATIONSHIP OF LETTERS

sans serif, trying the same or different configurations until you feel satisfied with at least two solutions.

Draw the image on an 8 x 8" piece of smooth-surface illustration board, leaving about 1½" surrounding the image from the edge of the board. Render the image in black India ink, using a ruling pen or technical pen for the outline and a brush to fill in the outlined areas.

THE RELATIONSHIP OF LETTERS ASSIGNMENT

The first letter of your last name is your assigned letterform. Choose a type style and draw your letter. Trace or draw that letter three more times to form a configuration where the spaces between the letters come together to form a separate shape. The letterforms can touch one another but cannot overlap. Select two of your sketches and render each design in black ink on a piece of white illustration board 8 x 8".

In figures 30–36, strong shapes created by the negative areas of the letters and pleasing positive images suggest good possibilities for energy-related and business-oriented trademarks.

Figures 39 and 42 are examples of what can be done with *more than four* letterforms in a repeating configuration.

Materials needed

1. Tracing paper for sketching
2. Pencils for sketching
3. Type book or prestype catalogue
4. Technical fountain pen or ruling pen
5. Ink for pens

6. India ink
7. Brush
8. Smooth-surface illustration board

Reference

Craig, James. *Designing with Type.* New York: Watson-Guptill Publications, 1971.

Haley, Allan. *Phototypography.* New York: Charles Scribner's Sons, 1980.

Kuwayama, Yasaburo. *Trademarks & Symbols.* New York: Van Nostrand Reinhold, 1973.

Longyear, William. *Type and Lettering.* New York: Watson-Guptill Publications, 1966.

Ruder, Emil. *Typography.* New York: Hastings House, 1967.

Wildbur, Peter. *International Trademark Design.* New York: Van Nostrand Reinhold, 1979.

30 Thomas Tringale

31 Thomas Tringale

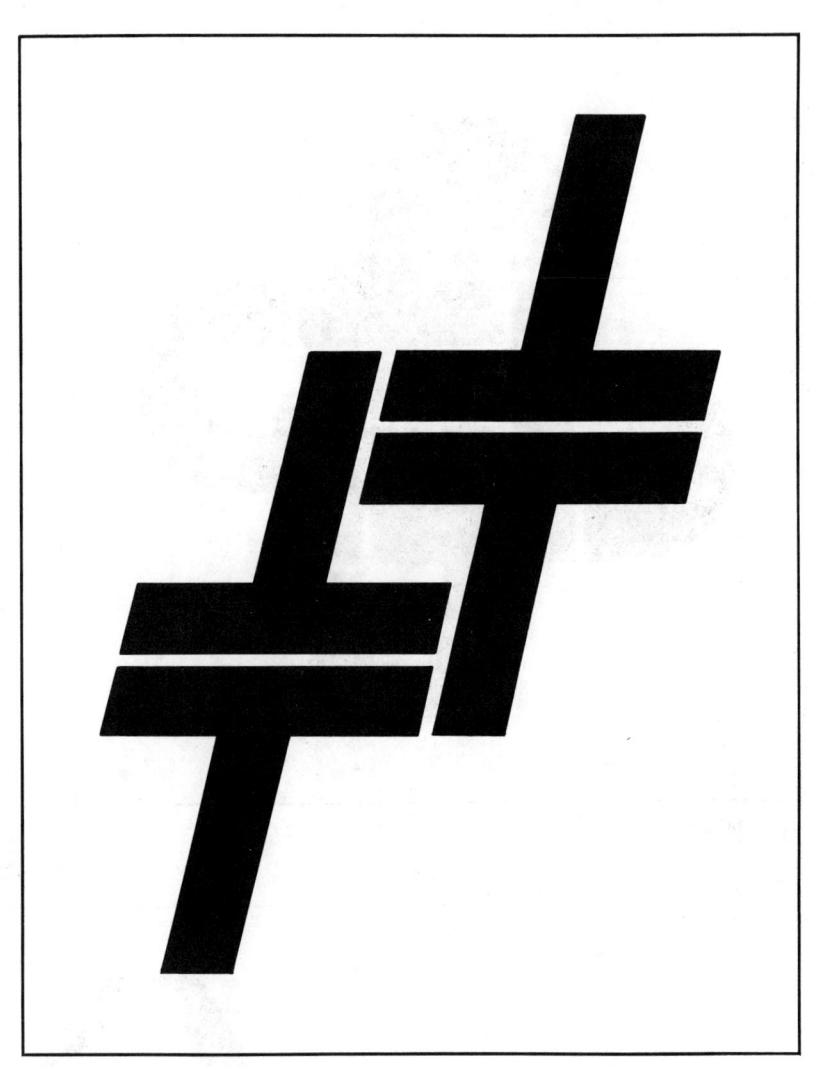

32 Thomas Tringale

33 Ed Malouf

34 Ed Malouf

35 Nancy Rider

36   Cindy Luecke

37   Dan Gee

THE RELATIONSHIP OF LETTERS

38   Tracy Wampler

39 Suzanne McCarthy

40 Elisabeth Rabinowitz

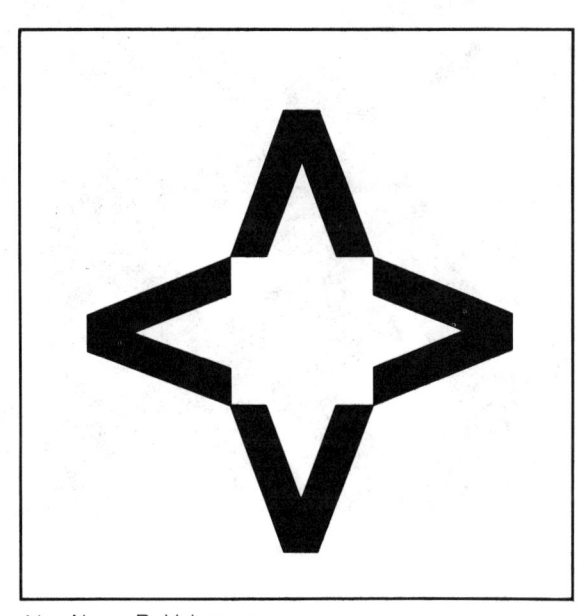

41 Alwyn R. Velasquez

THE RELATIONSHIP OF LETTERS

42 Ed Malouf

three
LETTERFORM PROGRESSIONS

Rhythm in its relationship to design can be defined as any visual pattern that causes the eye to move readily from one element to another. Rhythm as a design principle involves a clear repetition of elements that are the same or only slightly modified.

Progressive rhythm, or visual progression as I usually refer to it, involves the repetition of a shape that changes in a regular, fluid manner. This type of rhythm can be achieved with a progressive variation of the size of the particular shape from one motif into another. Each progressive step should be visually equal in its relation to the step preceding and to the next step in the sequence.

The number of steps required for a form to change from one situation to another determines the speed of the progression. When the steps are few, the speed becomes rapid (figure 43); when the steps are many, the speed slows (figure 44).

As with any given shape or form, the formal structure of a letterform can be manipulated to take on another identity or to create a new meaning through the use of visual rhythmic progression. We begin by using an assigned letterform (as in Chapter 2's assignment). In this case the letterform will be the first letter of your first name. The problem is to take that letterform and alter its structure in each successive step. You are building toward a predetermined object or recognizable form, which is completed in the ninth and final step of the visual progression.

The object you select should be in the form of a pictograph. A pictograph is a pictorial symbol representing an object (figures 45 and 46). The object and resulting pictograph should be simple, easily recognizable, and not difficult to achieve in a nine-step progression. The pictograph can be solid black or in outline form.

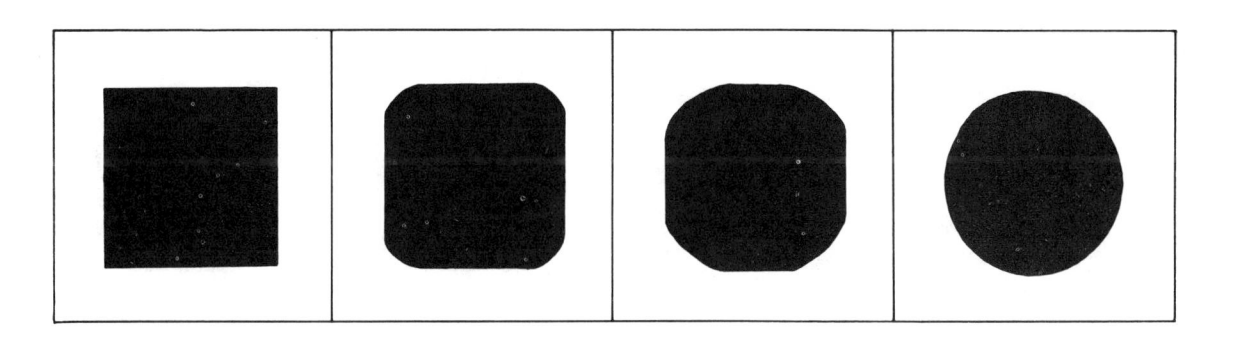

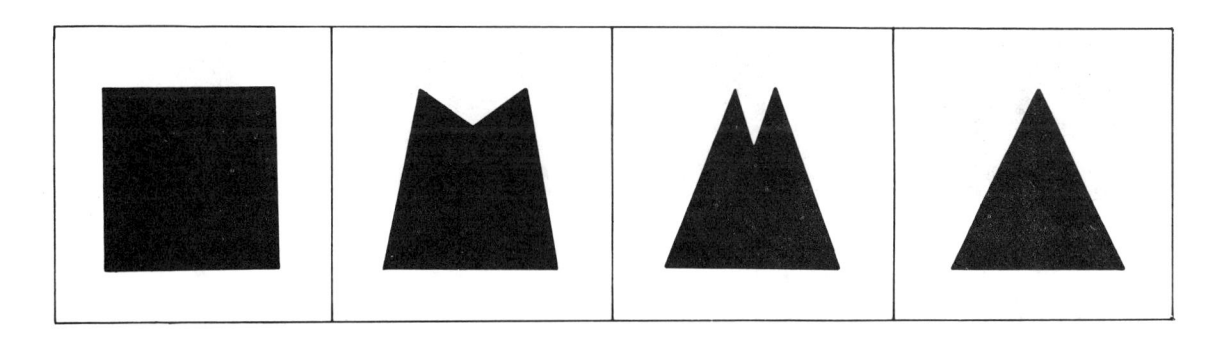

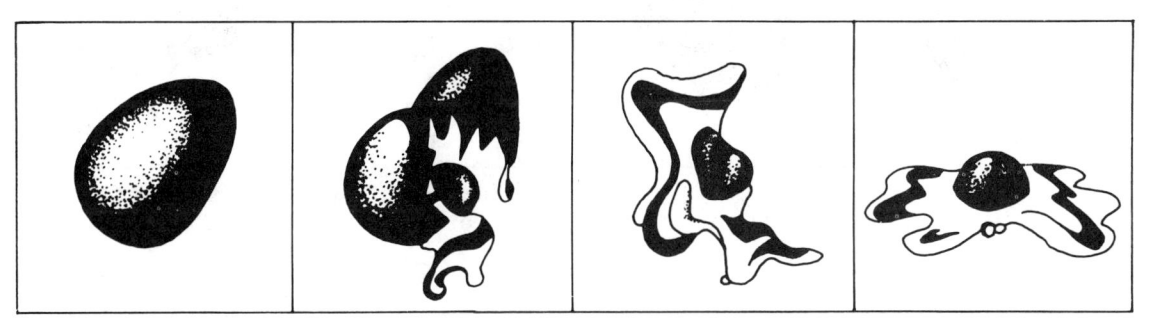

43 Suzanne McCarthy, Rapid progression

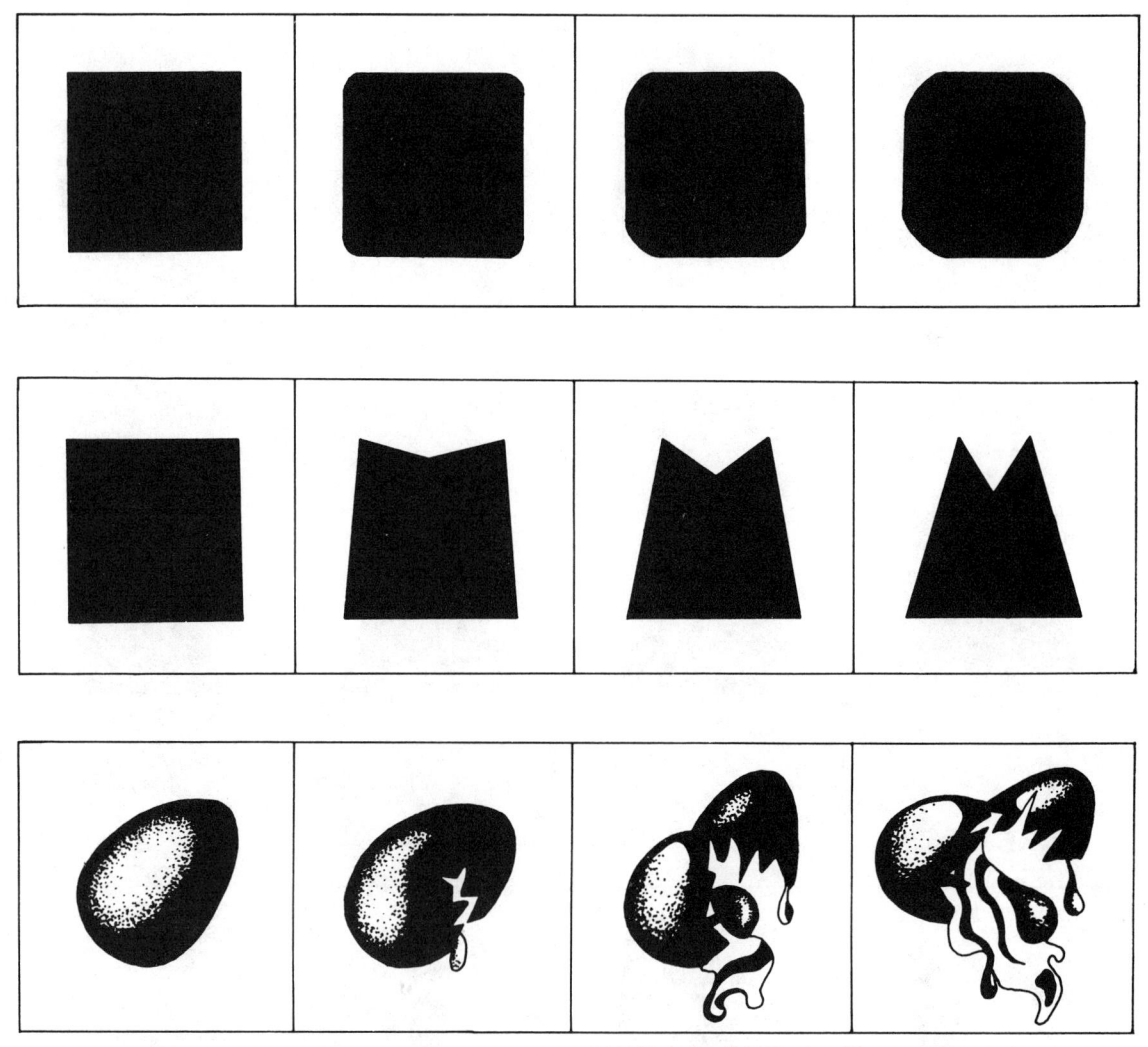

44 Suzanne McCarthy, Slower progression

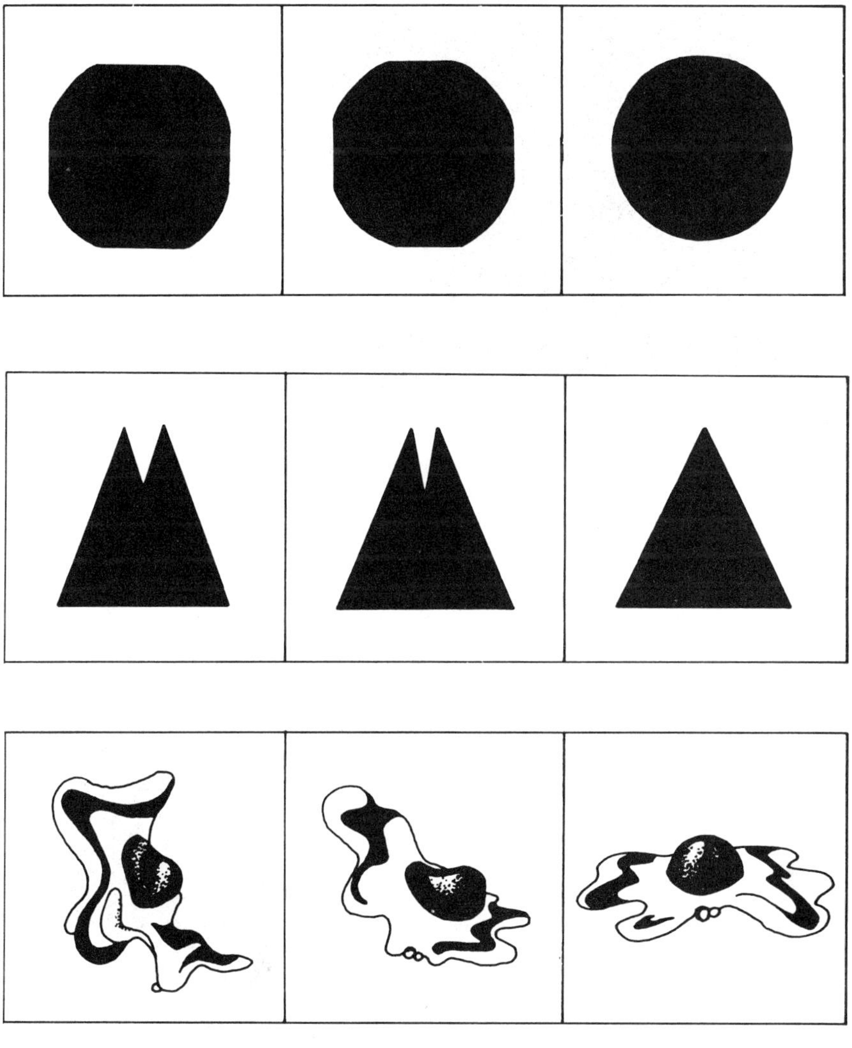

45 Symbol for coffee shop from the
American Institute of Graphic Arts system of
passenger/pedestrian-oriented
symbol program

46 Symbol for telephone from the
American Institute of Graphic Arts system of
passenger/pedestrian-oriented
symbol program

LETTERFORM PROGRESSIONS

In beginning this assignment, it is a good idea to first draw your object in the form of a pictograph; then choose a type style suggesting visual characteristics consistent with the pictograph so the transition will appear quite fluid. Once you have determined the letterform style and the object, draw nine boxes in sequence, each approximately one inch square. Place the letterform in box 1 and the object in box 9. Now begin to visualize the changes necessary to go from the letterform into the object. This process is called the thumbnail sketch. A thumbnail is a preliminary visual idea drawn quickly. You could say it is "thinking with your pencil."

While you are sketching in steps 2–8, please keep in mind that each step should not take larger visual jumps than the step preceding or the step to come. One way to test whether your progression has equal motion is to run your eye quickly from left to right through the progression. If your eye encounters a stop somewhere through the progression, examine that step to determine what seems out of place. Look at the step to the left and the step to the right. If necessary, rework the steps until you achieve a fluid eye motion when you look from the left to the right of the progression.

The finished artwork will be rendered on nine pieces of 6 x 6" smooth illustration board in black ink or black designers gouache. Hinge the nine panels on the back with masking tape ½" or more wide to achieve an accordion-folded effect (figure 47).

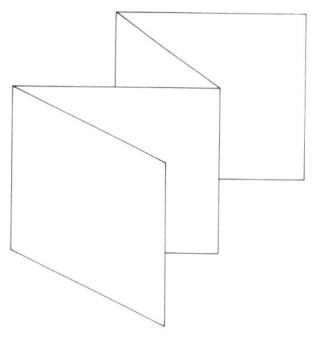

47 Accordion fold

THE LETTERFORM PROGRESSION ASSIGNMENT

This assignment is a visual progression of nine plates (steps). The first letter of your first name is your assigned letterform. The first plate will show your letterform in a selected type style. The ninth and final plate will show an object you have selected evolving from the letterform in plate 1. Steps 2–8 will be an equal visual progression of this evolution. The nine plates will be fitted together accordion-fashion to resemble a book.

Materials needed

1. Tracing paper for sketches
2. Pencils for sketches
3. Type book or prestype catalogue
4. Technical fountain pen or ruling pen
5. Ink for pens
6. India ink or black designers gouache
7. Brush
8. 9 pieces of 6 x 6" smooth illustration board
9. Masking tape ½" wide
10. Drafting materials (T-square, triangles, etc.)

Reference

American Institute of Graphic Arts. *Symbol Signs*. New York: Hastings House, 1981.

Cheatham, Frank and Jane. *Design Concepts and Applications*. Englewood Cliffs, N.J.: Prentice-Hall, Inc., 1983.

Dair, Carl. *Design with Type.* Toronto and Buffalo: University of Toronto Press, 1982.

de Sausmarez, Maurice. *Basic Design: The Dynamics of Visual Form.* London and New York: Studio Vista/Van Nostrand Reinhold, 1964.

Dreyfuss, Henry. *Symbol Sourcebook.* New York: McGraw-Hill Book Company, 1972.

Hofmann, Armin. *Graphic Design Manual.* New York: Van Nostrand Reinhold, 1965.

Lauer, David A. *Design Basics.* New York: Holt, Rinehart and Winston, 1979.

Longyear, William. *Type and Lettering.* New York: Watson-Guptill Publications, 1966.

Maier, Manfred. *Basic Principles of Design.* New York: Van Nostrand Reinhold, 1980.

McKim, Robert H. *Experiences in Visual Thinking.* Monterey, California: Brooks/Cole Publishing Company, 1972.

Meggs, Philip B. *A History of Graphic Design.* New York: Van Nostrand Reinhold, 1983.

Modley, Rudolf. *Handbook of Pictorial Symbols.* New York: Dover Publications, 1976.

Ruder, Emil. *Typography.* New York: Hastings House, 1967.

Wong, Wucius. *Principles of Two-Dimensional Design.* New York: Van Nostrand Reinhold, 1972.

48   Sharon Boisvert
This progression allows us to follow the gradual development of the letter S as it separates into two evolving fish forms.

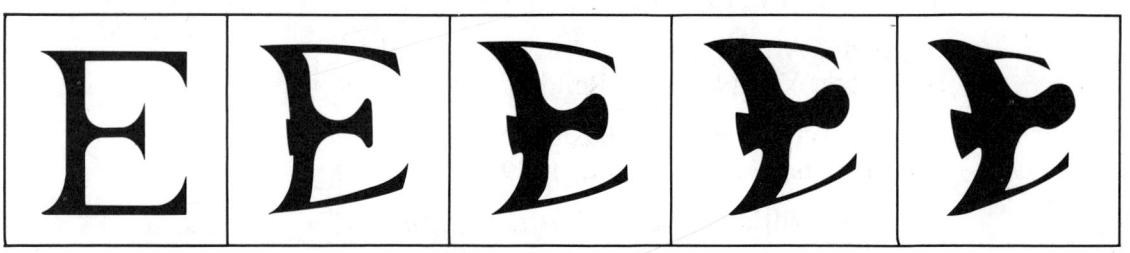

49   Ed Malouf
Here we see the student compressing and expanding his letter E into a bird in flight. His progression is reminiscent of an airplane retracting its landing gear in flight.

50   Janet Palasek
In this particular lowercase "j" we will find all the essentials available for the student to obtain a smooth progression from the letter into a circus seal.

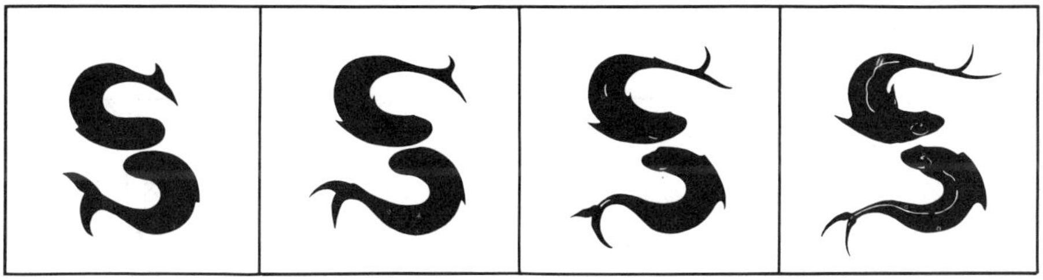

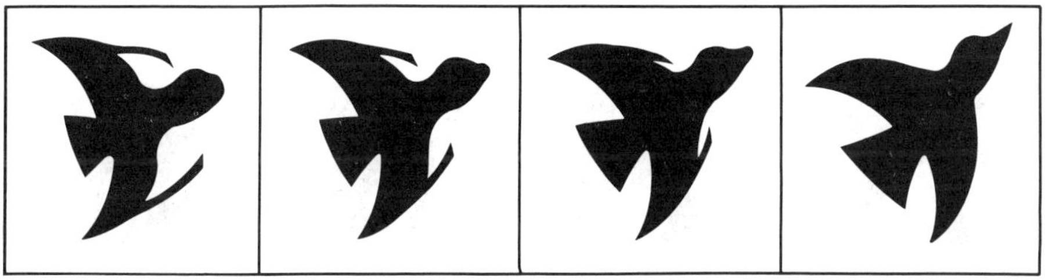

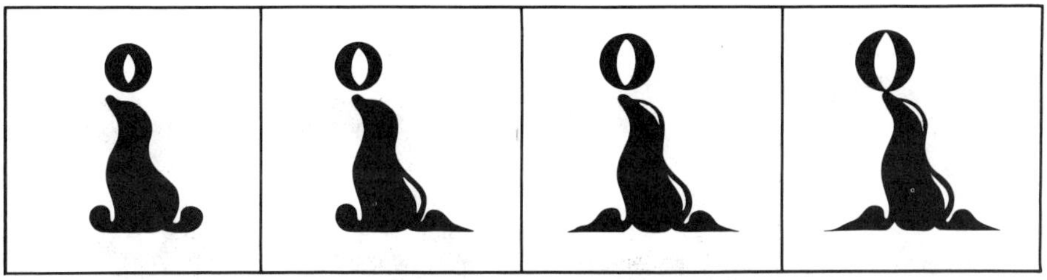

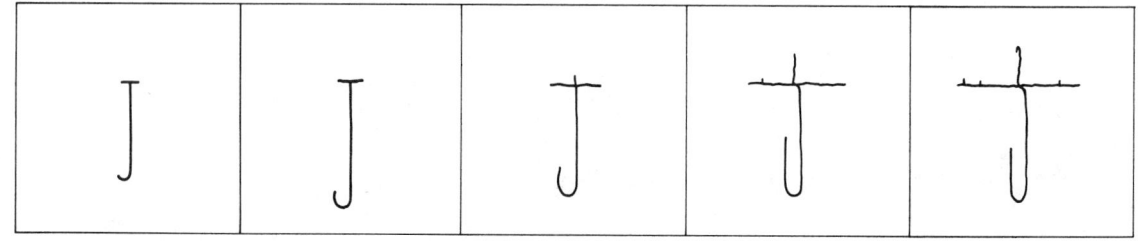

51 Julie Pavone Barron
This study shows the organic growth from a hand-drawn letter J into a carrot. I find it particularly pleasing to watch the piece develop.

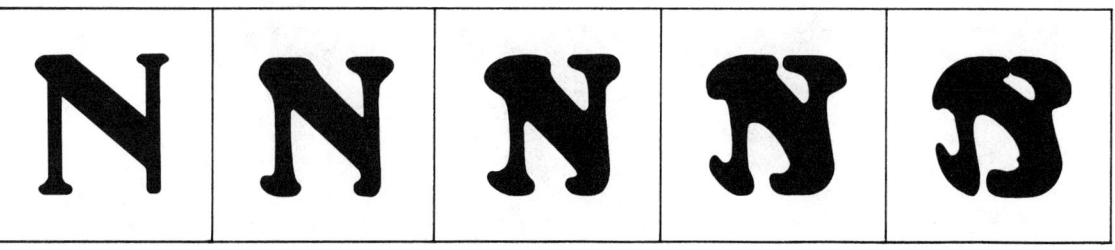

52 Nancy Pettibone
In this study, make note of how the student utilizes the negative spaces of her letter N to create the important highlights necessary to form a telephone.

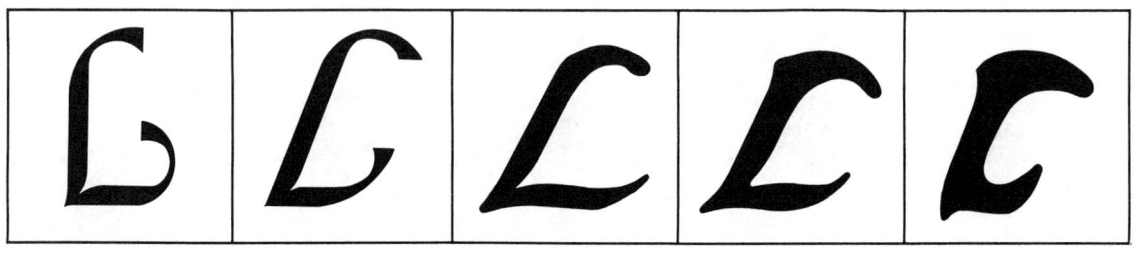

53 Lynne Ramirez
The negative shapes created by the evolving L are as interesting as the stretching of the L into a flying fish illustration.

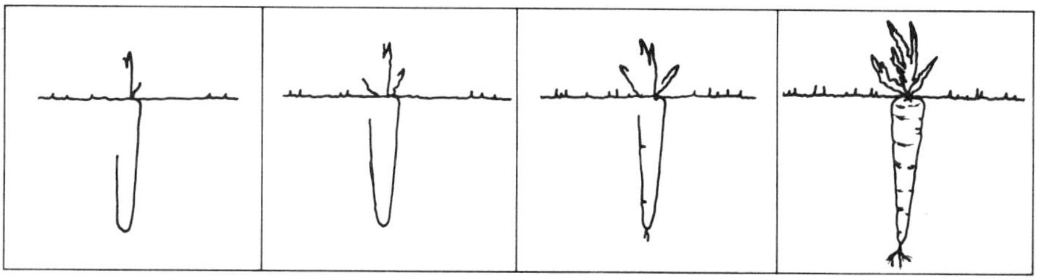

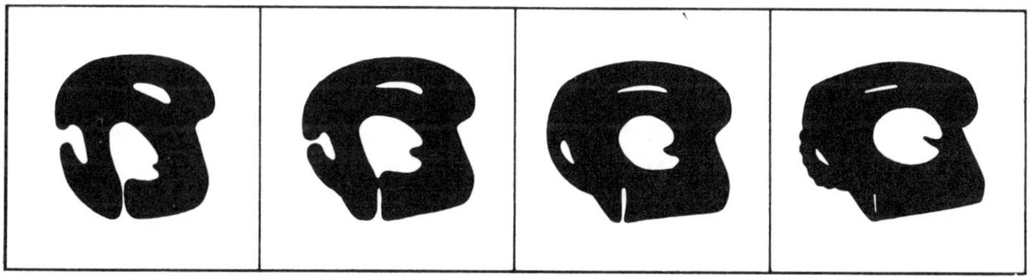

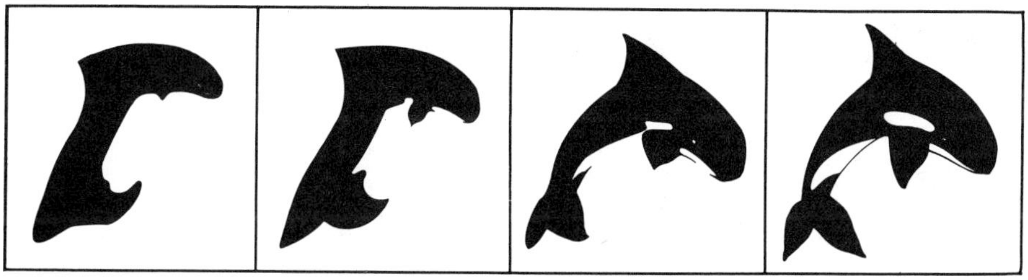

four
WORD ACTION PROGRESSION

| SMILE | SMILE |

54 Linda Cheren

When using typographic forms to communicate an idea or message, it is the designer's job to catch the viewer's attention and provide an imaginative design that stimulates the viewer by offering some kind of visual satisfaction. In this chapter we will explore illustrative typography using visual progression as a means to the solution.

Illustrative typography is a form of illustration in which letters and words are arranged to convey the particular word's visual meaning. The placement of the letters in a word may function more dramatically than straight text simply by manipulating the letterforms to create an interesting, animated design. You must remember that the physical structure of typography is made up of words, and typographic form depends on the nature of the words used. It is important that a chosen word have something to communicate and do so with direct simplicity (see figure 54).

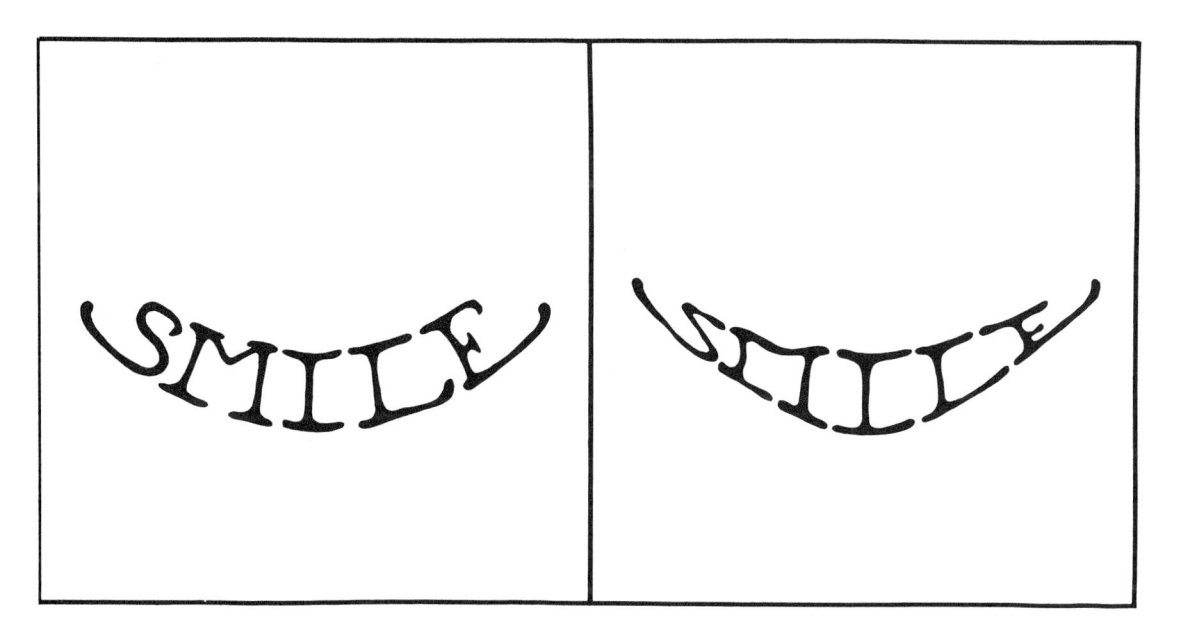

To begin this assignment, we will need to find a word that can lend itself to a visual meaning. Make a list of words that denote or describe an action. The first words on your list will probably be "hop," "skip," "jump," "run," "jog," etc. It is fine to put these first thoughts down at the top of the list to clear your mind of them. Now begin to think of more complex action words. You may use a dictionary to help you form your list. To make this assignment a challenge, you will need to focus on a visually challenging word—one that describes an action but offers no easy visual solution.

After you have compiled a list of twenty to thirty words, look each word over and try to visualize an illustration that uses only the letters of the word. As this assignment is also a visual progression, you need to visualize a five-step process. The word will be introduced in the first plate unmanipulated, and as the progression proceeds through steps 2–5 the action and the meaning of the word take form. In step 5, the transformation should be complete, yet the word must be readable in order to have a successful solution. The fifth step must be able to stand on its own as a complete communication. The other four steps exist to show the evolution of the idea and how it was achieved.

After reviewing your list of words, select about six of them. On your layout paper draw five boxes in sequence, each approximately 1 x 1", or 1 x 1½" if you need your area to be more rectangular because of the length of the word. Begin to visualize the sequence your word is to take and sketch it in the appropriate box. Remember that each step or action should be visually equal. Select the strongest solution from the six sketch ideas and draw it full size (8 x 8" or 8 x 10") on your layout paper. Once your drawing is perfected, transfer the sketch on to the five pieces of illustration board (cut to the sizes mentioned above) using graphite tracing paper. This paper is specially treated with carbon graphite for easy transferring of an image onto another surface. Now render the image in black ink or black designers gouache. Hinge the five panels together on the back with masking tape ½–¾" thick for an accordion-folded effect (see figure 47 in Chapter 3).

THE WORD ACTION PROGRESSION ASSIGNMENT

Choose a word that describes an action. Then select or design a type style that "feels" or "describes" the action. The end result is five plates: in

WORD ACTION PROGRESSION

the first plate put your word in the chosen type style, and proceed in the next four plates to let the word visually progress into the action or become the action. Render your five plates in black India ink or black designers gouache and hinge them together accordion-fashion.

Materials needed

1. Tracing paper for sketches
2. Pencils for sketches
3. Type book or prestype catalogue
4. Technical fountain pen or ruling pen
5. Ink for pens
6. India ink or black designers gouache
7. Brush
8. 5 sheets of illustration board cut to 8 x 8" or 8 x 10"
9. Masking tape ½" wide
10. Drafting materials (T-square, triangles, etc.)

Reference

Longyear, William. *Type and Lettering.* New York: Watson-Guptill Publications, 1966.

McKim, Robert H. *Experiences in Visual Thinking.* Monterey, California: Brooks/Cole Publishing Company, 1972.

Oxford American Dictionary. New York and Oxford, England: Oxford University Press, 1980.

Scott, Robert Gilliam. *Design Fundamentals.* New York: McGraw-Hill Book Company, 1951.

55 Nancy Pettibone, "Splotch"

56 Lynne Ramirez, "Tangle"

57 Maureen Fox, "Stretch"

SPLOTCH   SPLOTCH

Tangle   Tangle

STRETCH   STRETCH

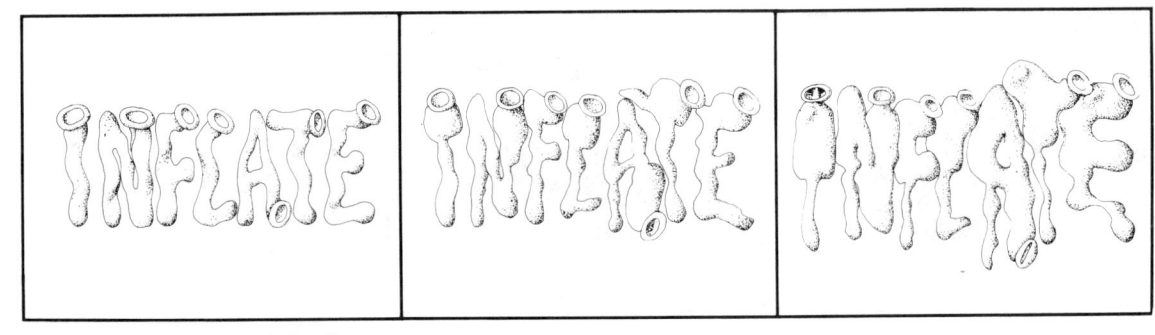

58 Mike Mullen, "Inflate"

59 Judith L. Pearson, "Congeal"

INFLATE INFLATE

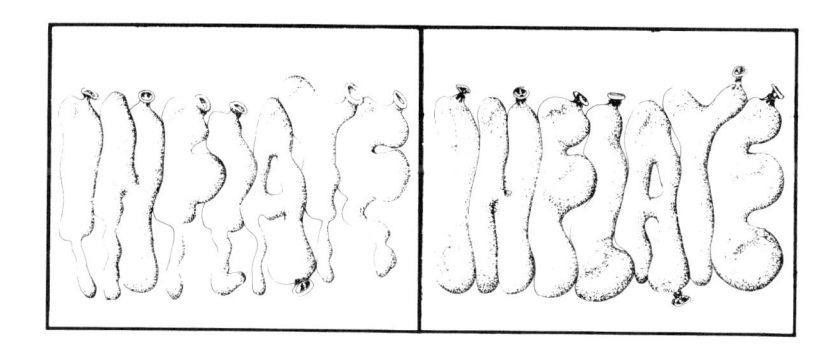

CONCEAL CONCEAL

five

WORD PLAY
TYPOGRAPHY

Some words can inspire their own visual solution, while others need more thought to bring about the ideas inherent in their meaning.

The designer can take a literal approach to a word's visual meaning (as in figure 60), a more playful attitude in the particular word's interpretation (as in figure 61), or an interplay of sound with meaning (as in figure 62). Ideas, as they reflect effective communication, must result from a careful thought process relating to the selected word's meaning, its symbols or symbolism in present-day language, and close observation of the structure of the letterforms making up the whole of the word.

Collating this information will probably suggest a direction from which you can draw your initial sketches. Most ideas will start with an abundance of parts, each part needing to be analyzed for its effectiveness in the resulting whole plus some streamlining of the essence of the idea into its simplest, and therefore most direct, form.

The first step in this assignment is similar to the word action progression assignment—we make a list of words. This particular list can show words representing any action, object, or noun inspiring or describing a visual solution. After listing your words, a good starting point is to look up their meanings in a dictionary. Most words have several language implications and you will have to choose one to bring forth in your visualization. Let's look at the word "struggle" (figure 63). The meaning, simply put, can imply a vigorous physical effort to overcome an opponent, a contest, or making one's way or living with difficulty. The student decided to show the visual interpretation of physical combat by positioning the two "g"s in

60 Abraham Seltzer
From *Typography* by Aaron Burns, Reinhold
Publishing Company, 1961

61 Lester Teich
From *Typography* by Aaron Burns, Reinhold
Publishing Company, 1961.

(fo-
net'
ics)

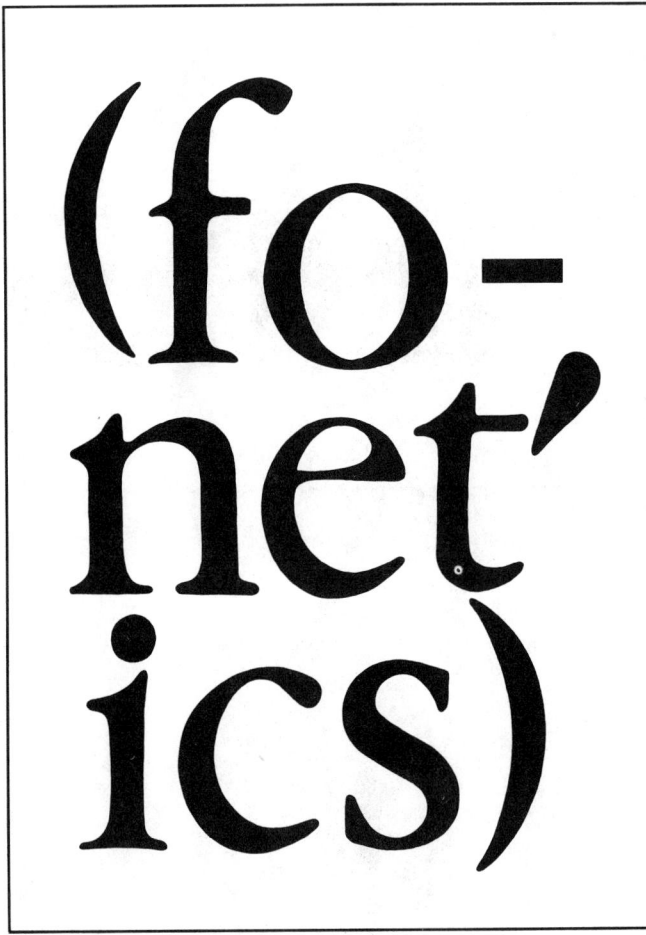

62 Colleen Marie Harquail

strugglе

63 Debra Salvucci

WORD PLAY TYPOGRAPHY

conflict with one another. Although the two "g"s are technically not readable in view of their superimposed positioning, the overall impact of the word suggests its meaning and results in its being legible.

Work with one word at a time, trying alternative visual ideas. Make your final sketch selection based on the simplest visual statement you are able to achieve. Render the solution on 15 x 20" illustration board, using black India ink or black designers gouache with a ruling pen and brush, or a technical fountain pen with black ink. Be sure to leave adequate white space surrounding the visualization on your illustration board.

THE WORD PLAY TYPOGRAPHY ASSIGNMENT

Choose a word and interpret its meaning typographically, using existing typefaces or a type design of your own. Render your design in black India ink or black designers gouache on 15 x 20" illustration board.

Materials needed

1. Tracing paper for sketches
2. Pencils for sketches
3. Type book or prestype catalogue
4. Technical fountain pen or ruling pen
5. Ink for pens
6. India ink or black designers gouache
7. Brush
8. 1 sheet of 15 x 20" illustration board
9. Drafting materials (T-square, triangles, etc.)

Reference

Burns, Aaron. *Typography.* New York: Reinhold Publishing Company, 1961.

Oxford American Dictionary. New York and Oxford, England: Oxford University Press, 1980.

Roget's International Thesaurus, 3rd ed. New York: Thomas Y. Crowell Company.

WORD PLAY TYPOGRAPHY

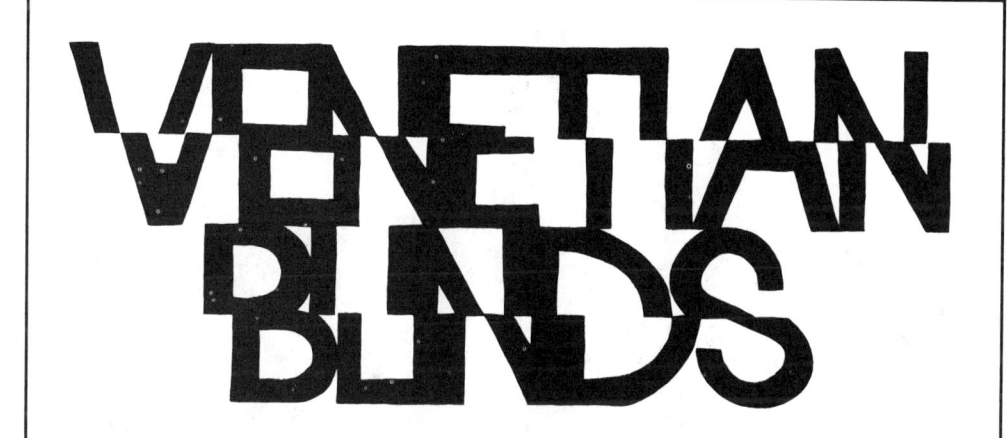

64 Miriam Wysoker, "Venetian Blinds"
This is a very appealing interpretation of an everyday object given life by the inventive use of the letterforms. I especially enjoy looking at the negative-shape areas created by the splits in the letters.

65 Barbara Apostol, "Neglect"
Here we see a more literal interpretation of the meaning of the word. It was achieved by separating the last letter from its core unit, showing the omission and separateness associated with the word "neglect."

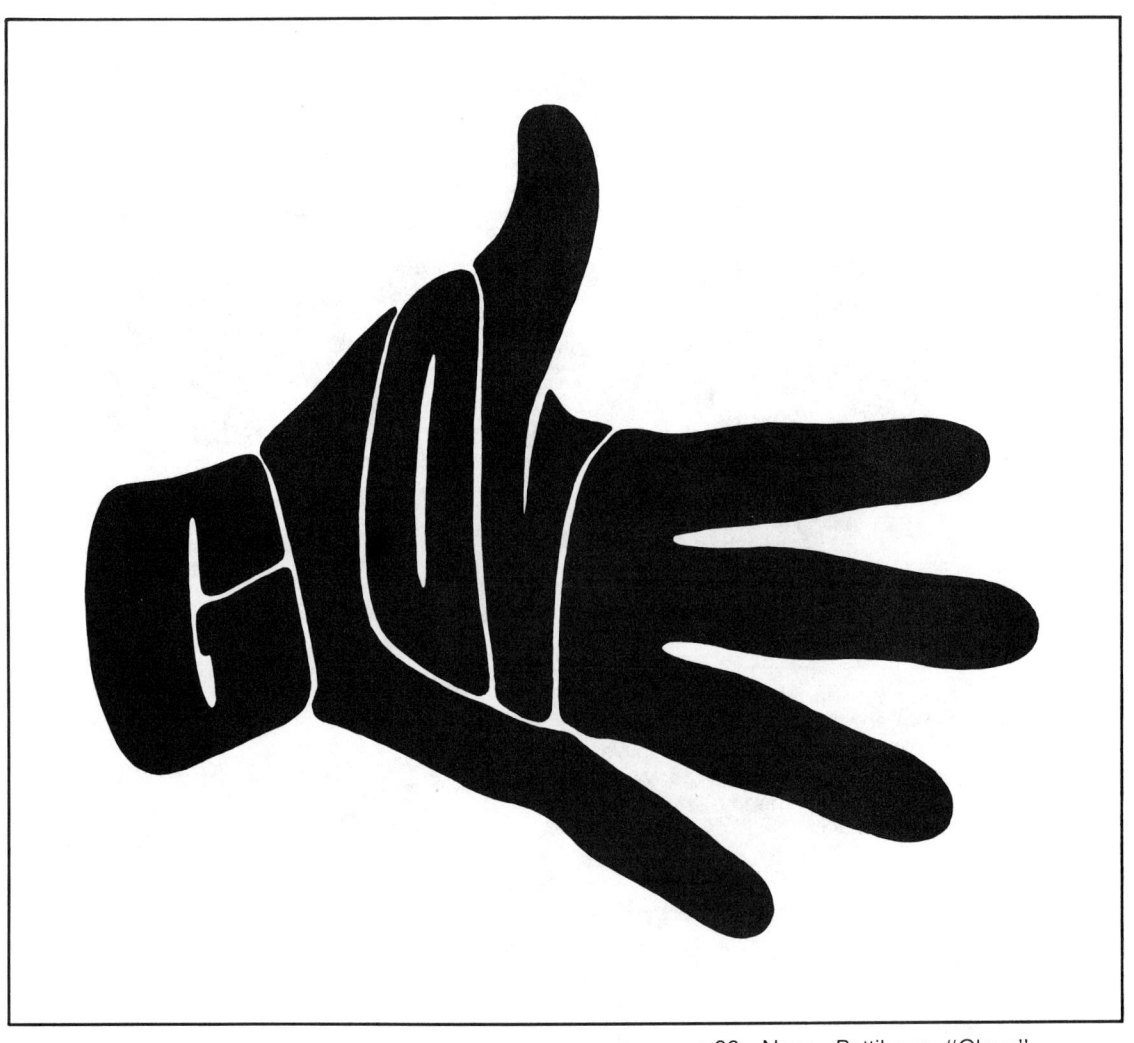

66 Nancy Pettibone, "Glove"
In this clever study, the student chose to represent an everyday object in a pictographic sense. The skillfully designed letterforms are molded into the individual finger shapes—and yet notice how well the entire study works as a unit to portray the single idea of a glove.

WORD PLAY TYPOGRAPHY

67 Ed Malouf, "Neurosis"
To achieve this exciting visualization, the student made vertical cuts through each italicized letter and reassembled the strips in a different arrangement. The equidistant parallel lines were then drawn to complete the unit and add to the student's interpretation.

68 Jean Albanese, "Puppet"
A wonderfully simple yet substantially literal representation. Good rendering and a sense of design and rhythm add a sparkle of life to the word.

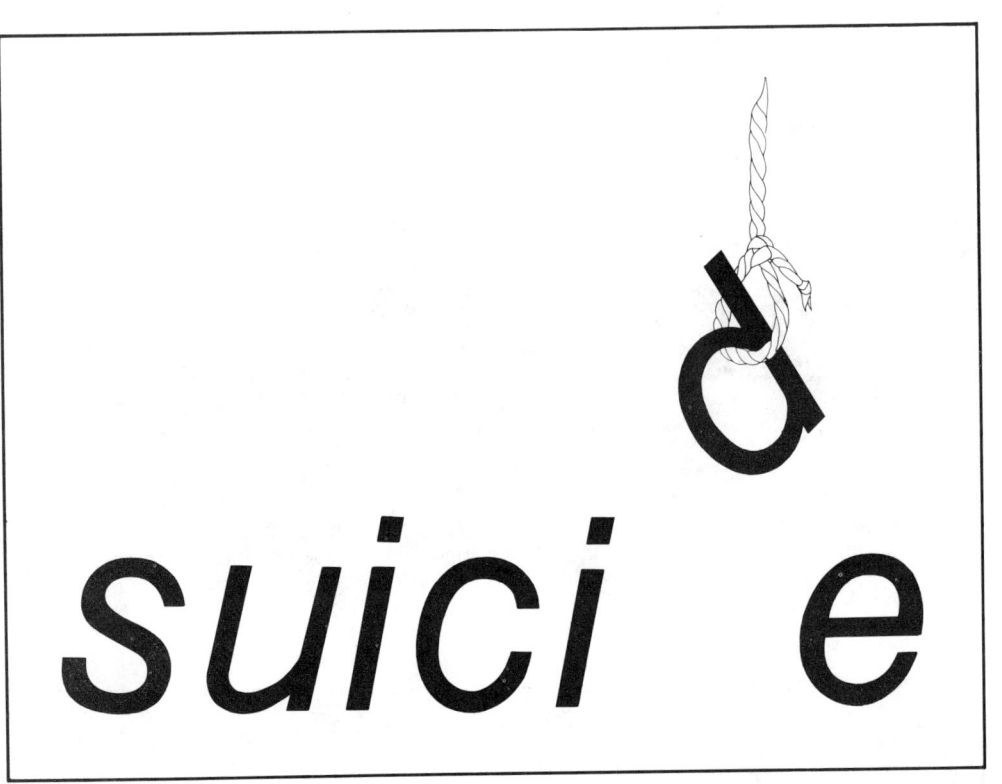

69   Andrea Shirley, "Suicide"
A humorous portrayal of a serious subject.
Its effectiveness is born of simplicity.

70   Luis-Miguel Muelle, "Shy"
The boldness of the letters "s" and "h"
overwhelm the fragile and cowering "y,"
which hides in the tunnel created by the
counter of the letter "h." A strong graphic
depiction of "shy."

six

SELF-PROMOTION TYPOGRAPHY

SELF-PROMOTION TYPOGRAPHY

Typography, when used as a tool, is capable of expressing any subject matter or emotion, be it humorous, factual, dramatic, inquisitive, direct, or illustrative. The range of expressions and meanings conveyed by typographic forms is limited only by the creative ability and imagination of the person applying them. Each designer formulates his or her own method of selecting appropriate imagery, in which the pictorial images created by personal association express some quality of the artist's mind.

Designing and formulating ideas for your own personal communication can be very challenging. You become the author of the problem's specifications: you state the problem at hand, analyze the data, draw up the basic parameters, and indicate a preliminary direction.

In the previous chapter on word play typography, you were asked to choose a word that could inspire its own visual solution or a solution you could create for it. In self-promotion typography you will use your first and last name to create a visual association with some aspect of your own identity. Your tools begin with a basic typeface— one you select or one of your own design. Of course, the problem goes beyond the acquisition of an appropriate typeface, since you need that all-important *concept* or idea on which to base your design. Some aspect of your personality, be it a physical attribute, a hobby or vocation, a personal cause, or visual statement (factual or humorous), needs to be discovered and then asserted. The selected idea is then incorporated with the typography, resulting in a unit that conveys essence of the visual association.

Look at figure 71, drawn by Gary Gibson. Gary is known for his warm, friendly smile. In this

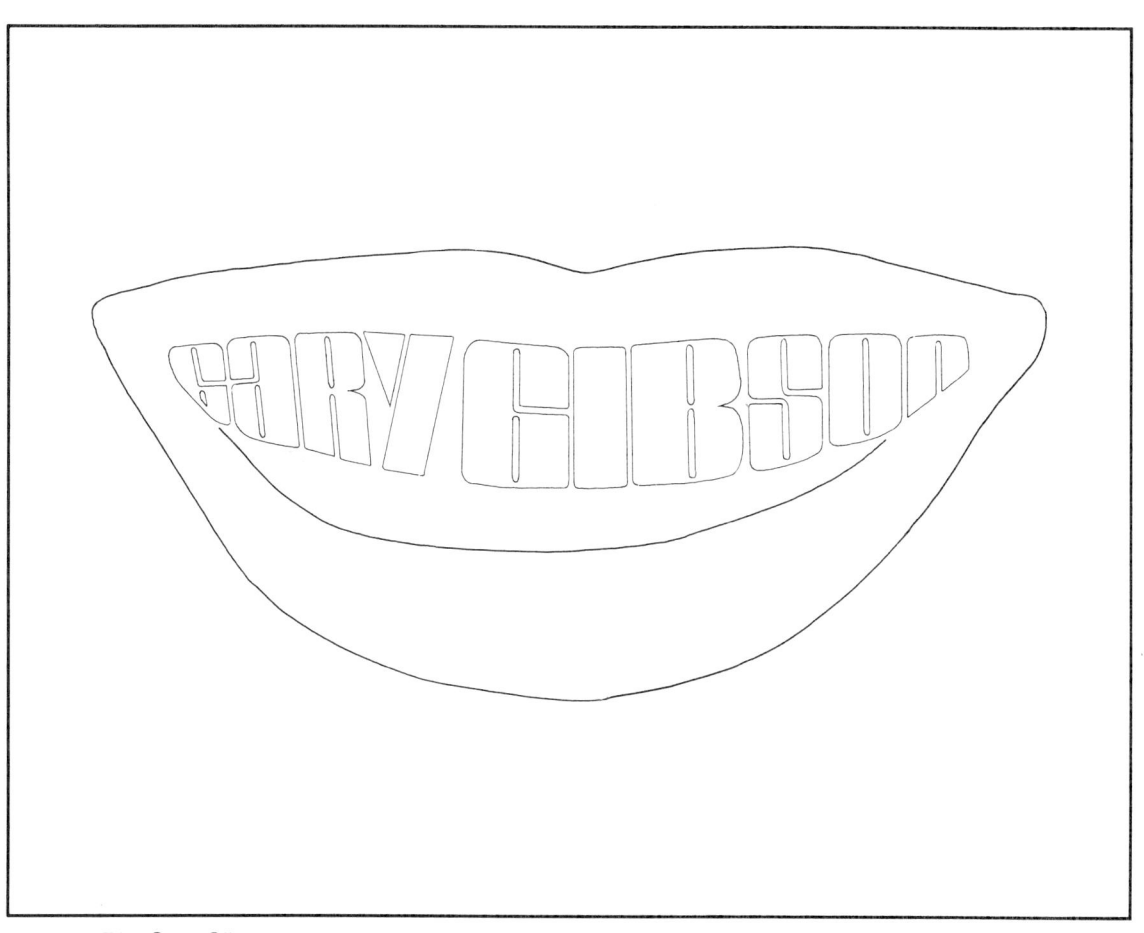

71 Gary Gibson

illustration, he is particularly skillful in rendering his name in typographic style that resembles teeth. The overall impact is a happy, friendly greeting.

In beginning this assignment, I suggest you make a list of your particular unique physical attributes, your interests, hobbies, or even your outlook on life. Now think—how can you best express *one* of the ideas on your list through the use of typographic forms? Without a solid idea on which to base your design, the result will be flat and without meaning, so I do suggest you not look at typefaces until the idea is clear in your mind. Draw or sketch a number of thumbnail visuals on several ideas before choosing one to draw up in large scale.

Use white illustration board, 15 x 20", and scale up your typography to fit in the center of the board with at least 2–3" of white space surrounding the design on all four sides. Carefully render your final design in black ink or black designers gouache using a rapidograph or brush.

THE SELF-PROMOTION TYPOGRAPHY ASSIGNMENT

Using your first and last name, design a typographic configuration expressing some aspect of yourself graphically.

Materials needed

1. Tracing paper for sketches
2. Pencils for sketching
3. Type book or prestype catalogue

4. Technical fountain pen or ruling pen
5. Ink for pens
6. India ink or black designers gouache
7. Brush
8. 1 sheet of 15 x 20" white illustration board
9. Drafting materials (T-square, triangles, etc.)

Reference

Berryman, Gregg. *Notes on Graphic Design and Visual Communication.* Los Angeles: William Kaufmann, Inc., 1979.

Hurlburt, Allen. *The Design Concept.* New York: Watson-Guptill Publications, 1981.

Typography 1: The Annual of the Type Director's Club. New York: Watson-Guptill Publications, 1980.

Typography 2: The Annual of the Type Director's Club. New York: Watson-Guptill Publications, 1981.

Typography 3: The Annual of the Type Director's Club. New York: Watson-Guptill Publications, 1982.

Scott Jeffery Gowan

72 Jeff Gowan
A student known by his middle name, Jeff has always had the task of informing teachers and fellow students of the name he wished to use. I find this a very playful clarification of his point.

Laura Jă′nŭs·kĕ′vĭch

73 Laura Januskevich
Having a particularly difficult last name to pronounce, Laura decided to use this as her concept and illustrate how her last name can be sounded out.

74 Margaret Langley
Here we see a beautiful piece of typography tied together by the use of transforming the "g" that is common to both her first and last names into a G clef which denotes her interest in music. The clue to the type of music Margaret is interested in (Renaissance music) is reflected in her choice of typography.

75 Katherine Diamond
A clever study by an editor turned design student. Using proofreader's marks, she edits her name.

76 Christopher Fortune
A student's passion for drinking beer is skillfully illustrated in this study.

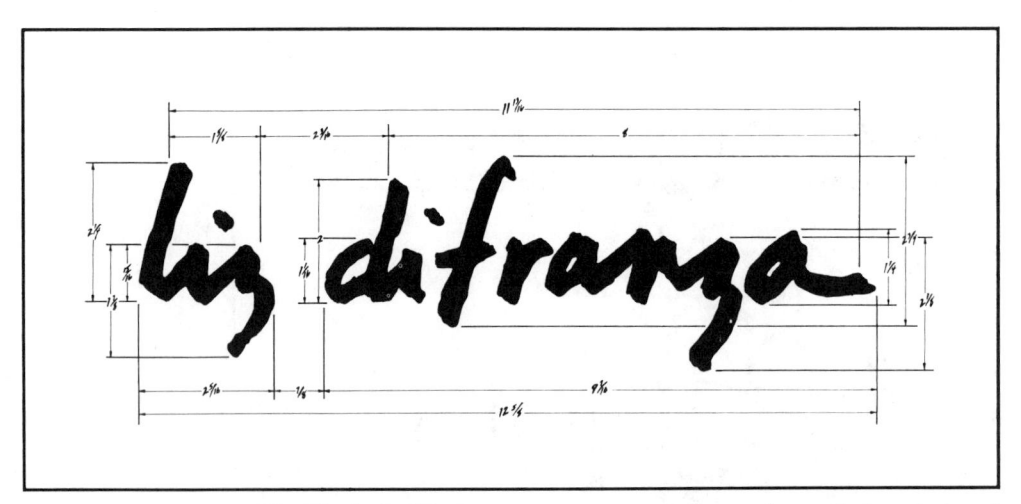

77 Elizabeth DiFranza
In this study, Liz is presenting an interesting juxtaposition of two important personal qualities reflected in her design work. She is very creative and open in her choice of ideas, which is denoted by the informal signature. However, Liz is very meticulous in the visual presentation of her ideas.

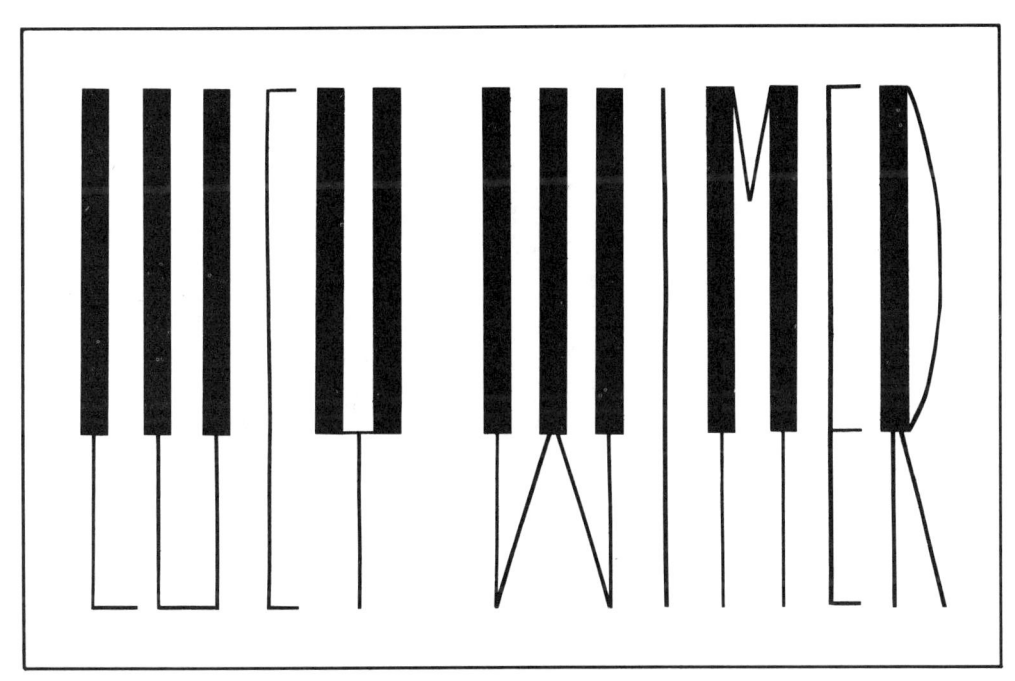

78 Lucy Wimer
A fun interpretation of Lucy's enthusiasm for
the piano.

79 Helga Hardy
The typography in this study, nicely drawn
and handsomely rendered, creates the
imagery of Helga's Germanic background.

$$\frac{m+a(r+i)}{r+(o+b^2)+a}$$

80 Maria Robba
Can you guess at Maria's interest? This piece is conceptually stunning with its use of lightweight typography in an algebraic configuration.

81 Tom Szumowski
The illustrator's answer to announcing an interest in photography.

seven
THE SIMPLE TOOL

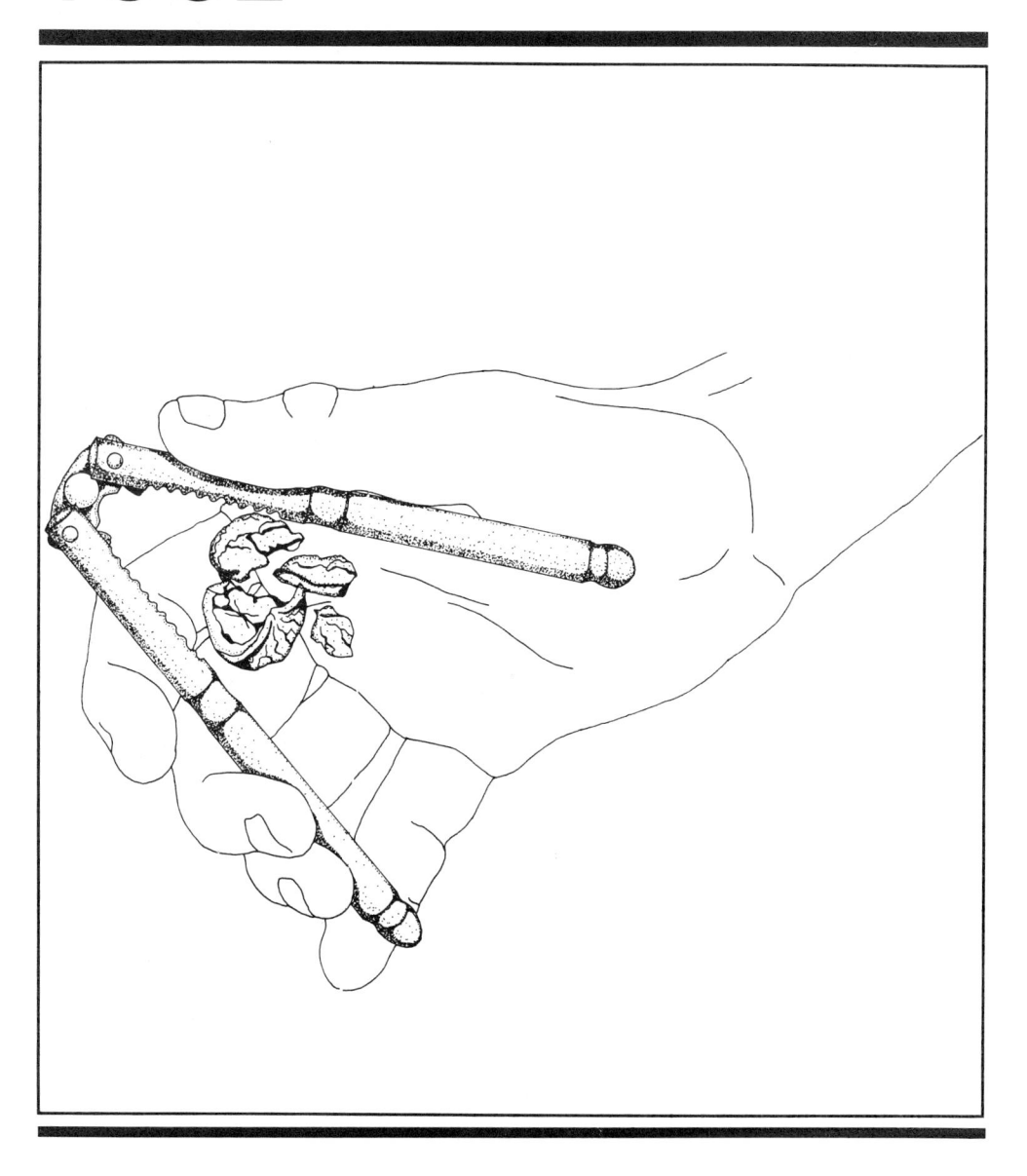

THE SIMPLE TOOL

In graphic design we use signs and symbols to educate as well as to inform. It is important for any student of design to learn how to take an everyday object like a can opener or hammer, observe it, and then draw the essential descriptive elements connected to the object's visualization in its simplest form. Once that has been accomplished, you will have a representational sign for the object. But that still does not necessarily describe the object's function or how a person would use the object in an ordinary situation.

In this particular assignment, I ask my students to choose an everyday simple tool—especially one they might take for granted because it is so commonplace. The student is then asked to study the object and commit to paper the necessary lines or shapes describing the three-dimensional object in two-dimensional language. It does not matter whether the object takes an outline form or a solid black shape. Once this has been accomplished, the student begins to describe how the object works, using five more steps in an equal visual progression to create a series. The simpler the demonstration, the better it is as an instructional device for the viewer. A good example is "Chopsticks" (figure 82). In this study, the student had to demonstrate the various hand positions necessary to successfully operate the two sticks as eating utensils.

When you begin to think about your selection of a simple tool, do not expend too much energy searching for an obscure or unusual tool. The intention of this exercise is to describe the functioning of any mechanical device in terms of a visual picture as a learning experience for the viewer.

For your initial sketches you will need to draw up six boxes (a double spread) in sequence,

THE SIMPLE TOOL

approximately 1 x 2" each. Begin as you did in Chapter 4 for the word action progression. Draw your object in box 1, then proceed to describe the action necessary in the subsequent boxes as you demonstrate the tool performing its function. The sixth box should show the outcome of the action.

Once you are satisfied with a set of working thumbnails, draw your idea full size on tracing paper to check scale and proportion. Render your final design on white illustration board cut in panels 8 x 8"; use a rapidograph if you are using black ink, or a brush and ruling pen if you are using black designers gouache. Hinge the six double spreads (twelve panels) together on the back side with masking tape to achieve an accordion-folded effect (see figure 47 in Chapter 3). Each 8 x 8" panel will show half of a double spread.

THE SIMPLE TOOL ASSIGNMENT

Choose a simple tool and design a book of six spreads (double pages) demonstrating the use of the tool or its function. Render in black and white.

Materials needed
1. Tracing paper for sketches
2. Pencils for sketches
3. Technical fountain pen or ruling pen
4. Ink for pens
5. Black designers gouache
6. Brush
7. 12 sheets of illustration board cut 8 x 8"
8. Masking tape ½" wide
9. Drafting materials (T-square, triangles, etc.) if necessary

Reference

American Institute of Graphic Arts. *Symbol Signs.* New York: Hastings House, 1981.

Dreyfuss, Henry. *Symbol Sourcebook.* New York: McGraw-Hill Book Company, 1972.

Hofmann, Armin. *Graphic Design Manual.* New York: Van Nostrand Reinhold, 1965.

Modley, Rudolf. *Handbook of Pictorial Symbols.* New York: Dover Publications, 1976.

Wong, Wucius. *Principles of Two-Dimensional Design.* New York: Van Nostrand Reinhold, 1972.

82 April Wong, "Chopsticks"
In this study, the student chose to create a solid form pictograph of hands and utensils for economy of information. An easy to follow guide on how to use chopsticks.

1
2
3
4
5
6

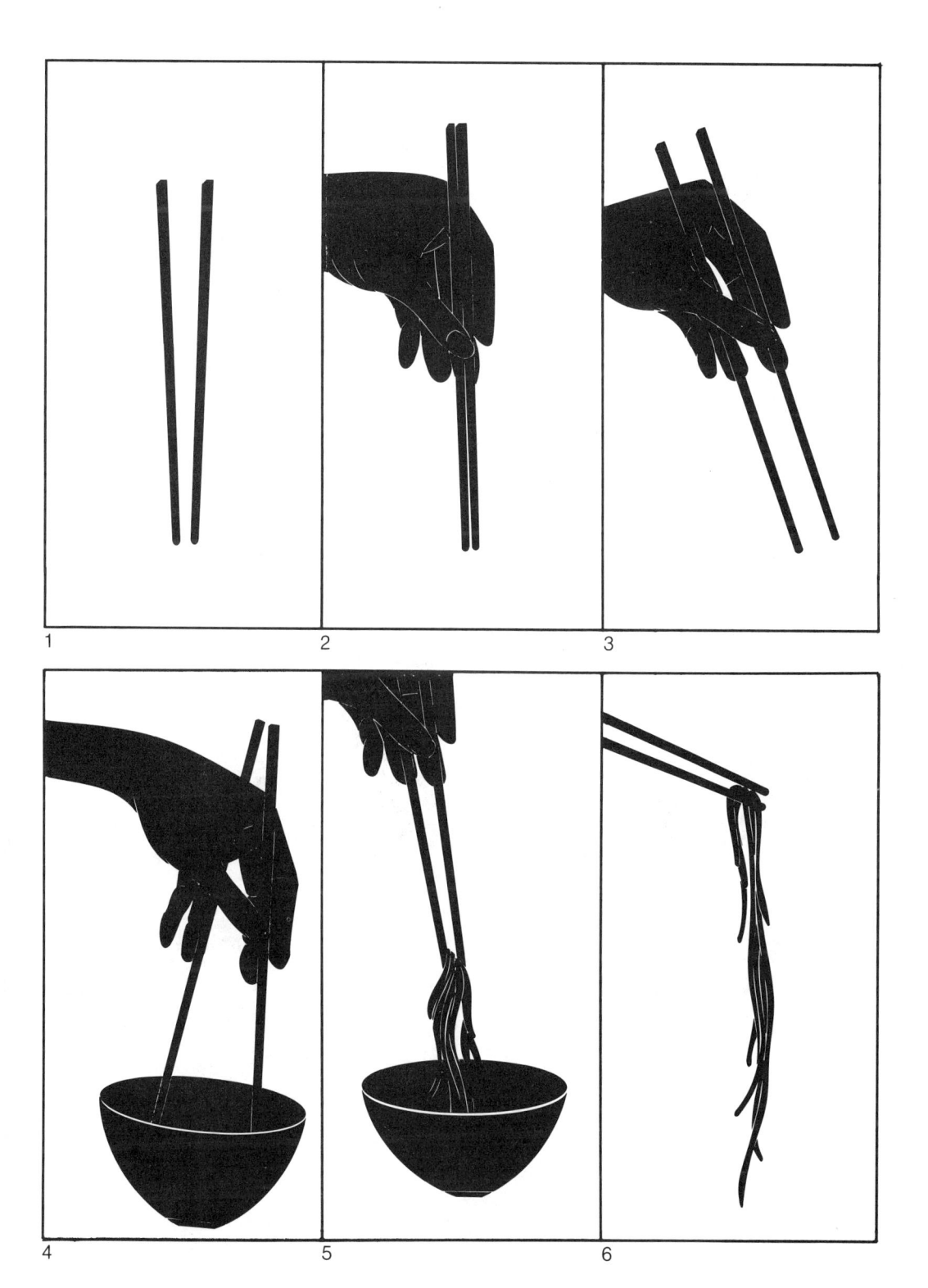

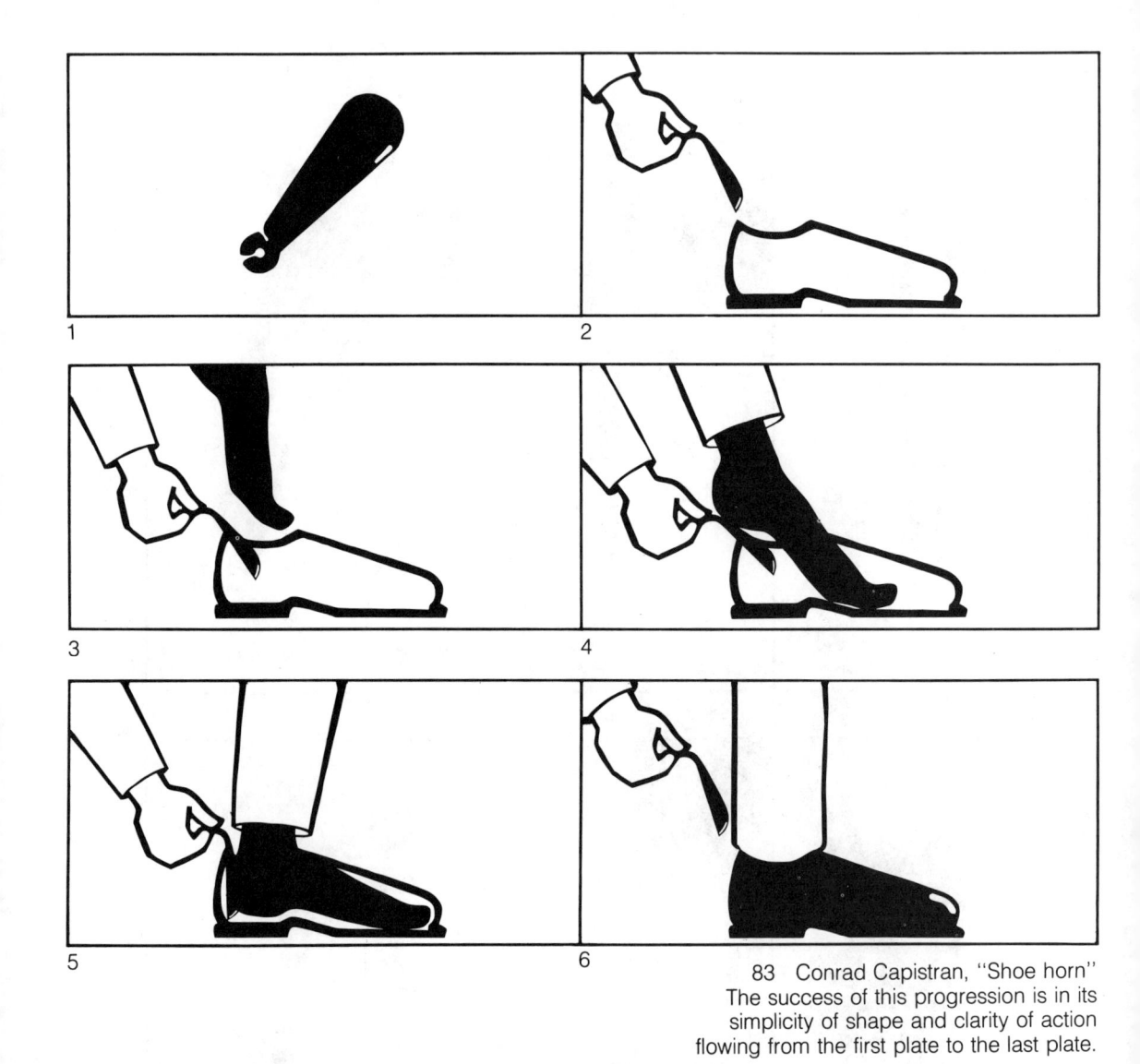

83 Conrad Capistran, "Shoe horn"
The success of this progression is in its simplicity of shape and clarity of action flowing from the first plate to the last plate.

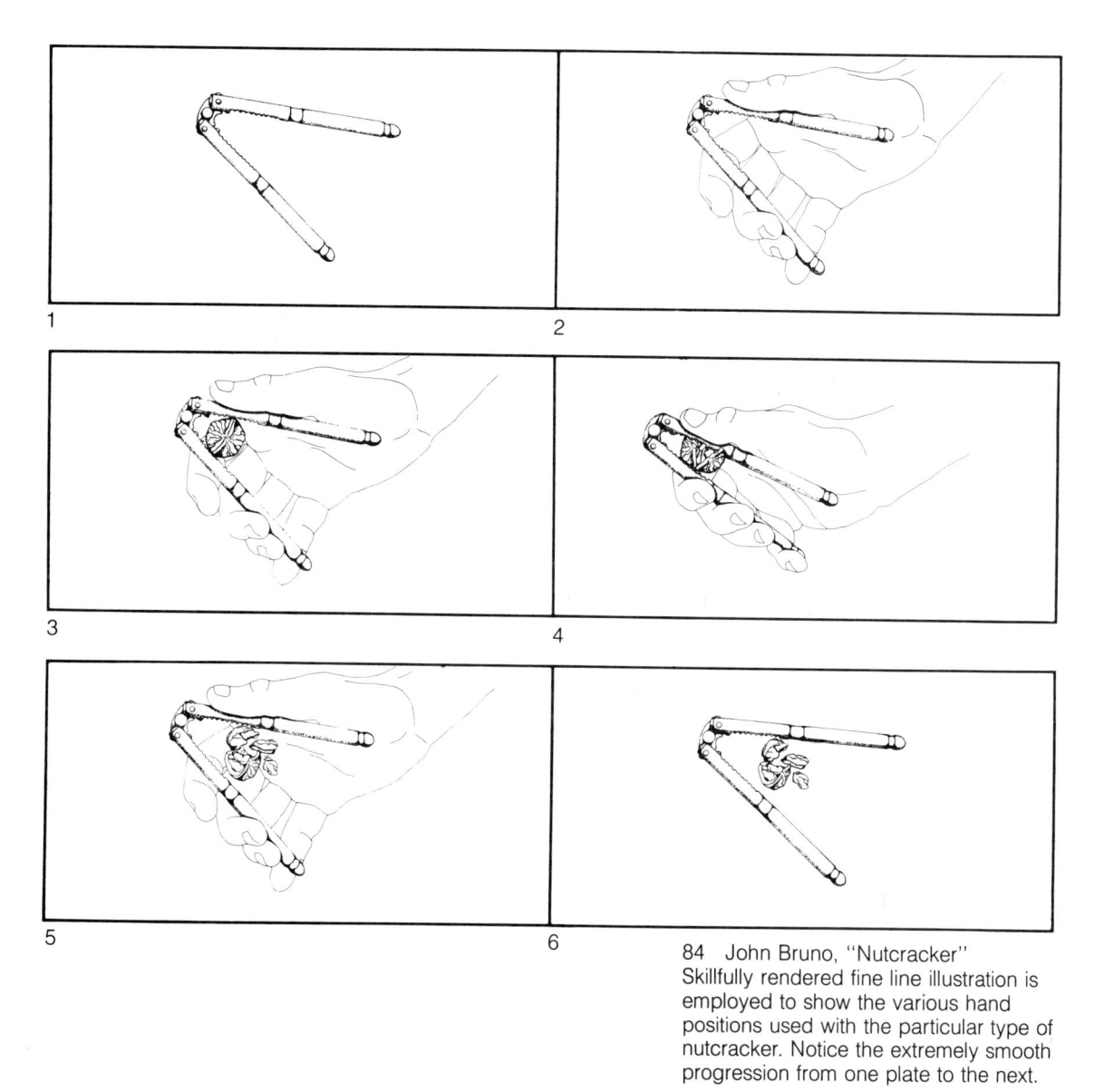

84 John Bruno, "Nutcracker"
Skillfully rendered fine line illustration is employed to show the various hand positions used with the particular type of nutcracker. Notice the extremely smooth progression from one plate to the next.

1

2

3

4

5

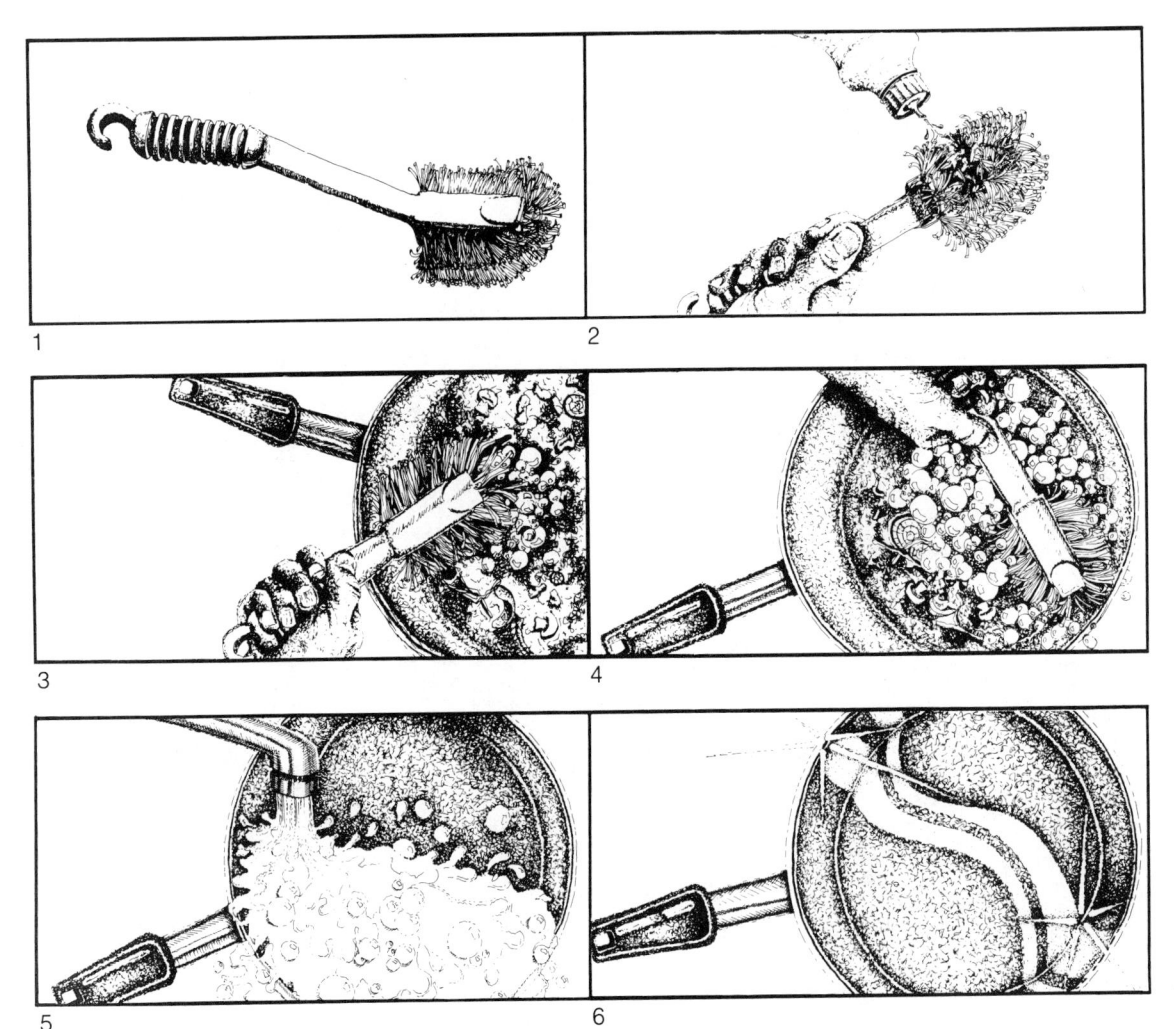

6

85 Mike Mullen, "Pot scrubber"
Another type of illustrative approach can be seen in this study. Shadowing and stippled pen work are used to create a fuller three-dimensional view of the tool and its function.

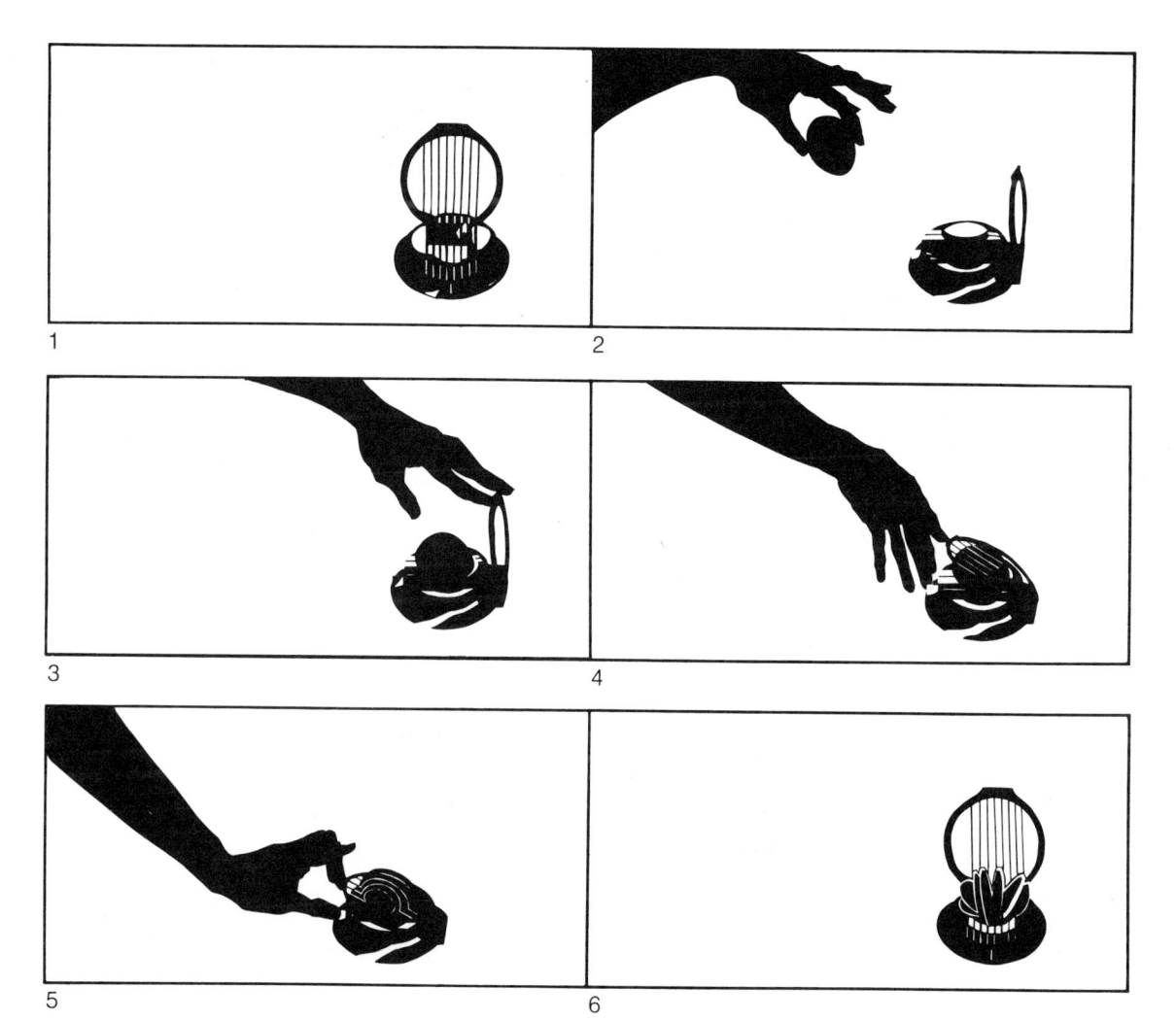

86 Sharon Boisvert, "Egg slicer"
Solid form pictographic shapes are
employed to demonstrate this simple tool
and the results of its use.

1 2 3 4 5 6

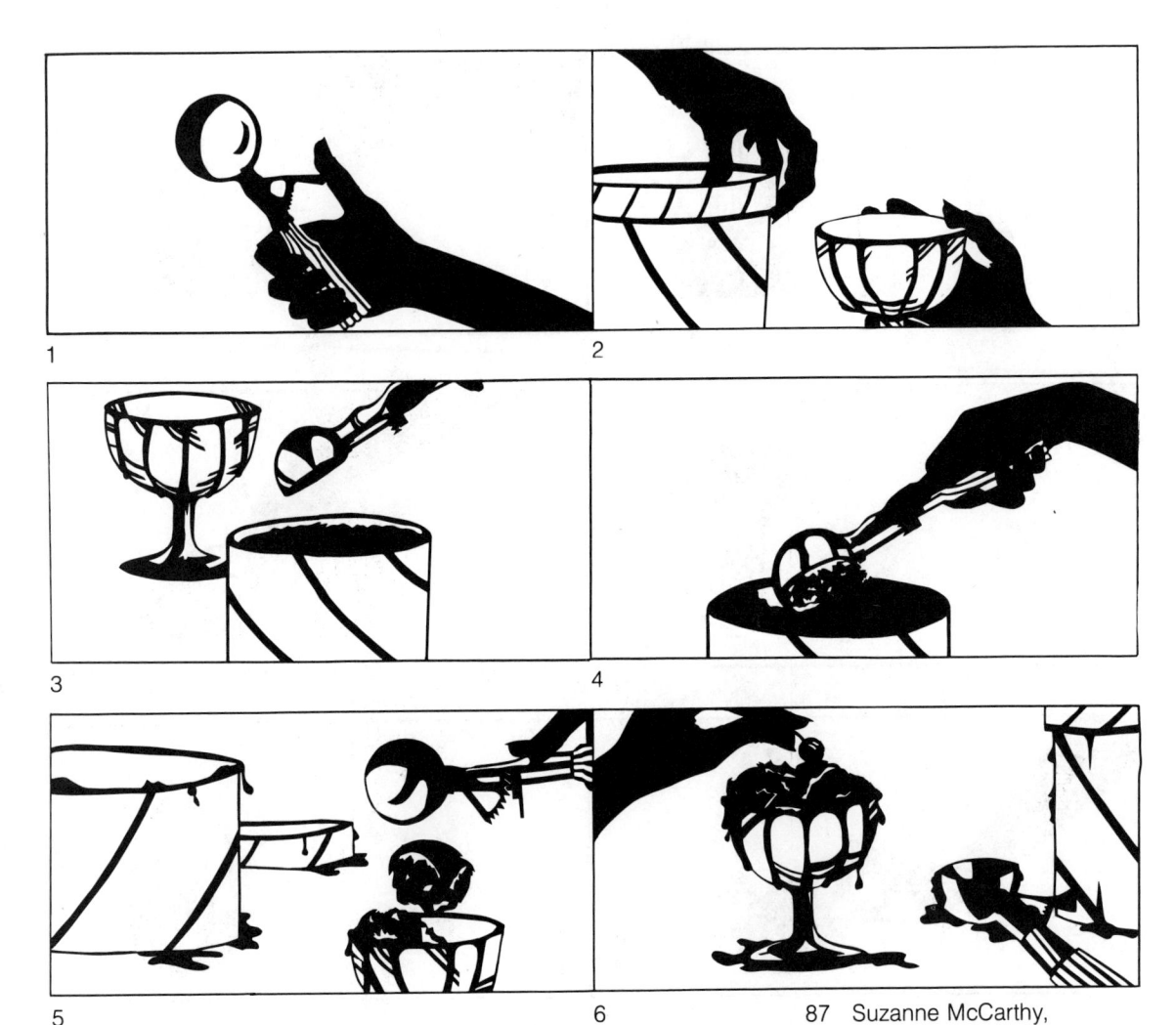

87 Suzanne McCarthy, "Ice cream scoop" This particular progression shows a bit of humor commonly experienced by the mess of scooping melting ice cream.

eight
THE QUOTE POSTER

The bank of friendship cannot exist without deposits

THE QUOTE POSTER

The poster has long been one of society's most useful forms of communication. The *American Heritage Dictionary* defines the poster as a large printed placard, bill, or announcement, often illustrated, posted to advertise or publicize something.

The increasing need to keep the public well informed has created expansion of this original utilitarian purpose into an aesthetic mode. A new visual vocabulary has been developed—one that heightens our awareness and design sensibilities while also enhancing our environment. Poster collecting, a trend begun in the early 1960s, has developed into an established market, with many galleries selling this "affordable art" to the many people who frame them for decoration in their homes and work areas.

As designers, our challenge is to take the desired message and create a visual vitality that is clearly projected when the poster is quickly scanned. A poster that does not read well does not do its job. In each of the preceding chapters, proposed visual exercises were designed so the student could experience the formation of ideas and develop visual awareness. In a poster these ideas will represent the given information. You can create outstanding visual performances from messages by learning an important key to poster composition: *how to interpret compositional space* (the way in which an image is positioned on a two-dimensional surface).

By definition, *composition* can be viewed as the total organization of any design. The participating forms and parts of forms in a composition have shape, size, and a position within the totality. The concept or idea is established through the relationships of these forms and their unique character of organization.

In this first of three poster assignments, we

THE QUOTE POSTER

are limited to typographic forms (utilizing a minimal amount of illustration if need be) to promote a chosen basic idea. The assignment in this chapter requires a selection of a group of related words in the form of a quote, saying, poem, song, or anecdote. Write the words down and examine them closely, seeking a key to guide you to a graphic pattern which will best express your interpretation of the quote's meaning. You will notice each grouping of words can take on a feeling or mood, which might suggest an initial form, layout, type style, and/or visual twist.

I suggest you select material that you personally enjoy. This will make it more challenging to you when you are searching for the best visual identity for your poster. Strive to keep your visualizations simple and easily understood. A good example to follow is the poster "Angels can fly because they take themselves lightly" (figure 97). In this particular poster, it is easy to analyze how the idea was formed. First, the designer created a cloudlike appearance in the copy by choosing a whimsical type style and then grouped the words, cut out of white paper, against a sky blue background. In the composition the "cloud of copy" is positioned high in the upper portion of the poster to create a floating sensation, which forms the important key element to the meaning of the chosen phrase.

The assignment calls for a 15 x 20" or 20 x 30" format, either horizontal or vertical. The letters need to be carefully cut out from Pantone® or Color-Aid papers, then positioned and glued on to colored mat board or board with a full sheet of colored paper already adhered to it. If you are pasting paper to paper or paper to board, remember to coat each surface with a thin layer of rubber cement, let dry, then put the surfaces together.

THE QUOTE POSTER ASSIGNMENT

Choose a quote, saying, song, poem, or anecdote and interpret its meaning typographically using the form of a poster. A minimal amount of illustration may be used to enhance the typographic design.

Specifications

Copy: the chosen quote

Size: 15 x 20" or 20 x 30", horizontal or vertical

Media: cut paper; no color restriction

Materials needed

1. Tracing paper for sketches
2. Pencils for sketches
3. Color-Aid and/or Pantone® art papers
4. X-acto® knife and extra blades
5. Type book
6. Rubber cement and pick-up
7. 15 x 20" or 20 x 30" illustration board

Reference

Burns, Aaron. *Typography.* New York: Reinhold Publishing Company, 1961.

Communication Arts Magazine. Palo Alto, California, published bimonthly.

Felde, Nathan, and Julius Friedman. *Public Works.* Louisville, Kentucky: Hawley, Cooke and Orr, Publishers, 1980.

Hurlburt, Allen. *The Grid.* New York: Van Nostrand Reinhold, 1978.

U&lc, The International Journal of Typographics. New York: International Typeface Corporation, published quarterly.

88 Brian Stanlake, "Every snowflake in an avalanche pleads not guilty."
Movement and form play important roles in this poster's visualization.

89 Cynthia Mulligan, "The road to success is always under construction"
The student's successful idea is based on the familiar shape of a pyramid under construction.

Never hyphenate the word headache unless it's a splitting one.

90 Pat Domenicucci,
"Never hyphenate the word headache unless it's a splitting one"
The concept here is a humerous play on the words "splitting headache." A very witty yet simple typographic solution.

People will only walk on you if you lie down first

91 Barbara Apostol,
"People will only walk on you if you lie down first"

Positioning the letter "e" on its back in the word "lie" gives emphasis to the message.

time: *n.* the (.) during which something happens.

92 Morella Caycedo,
"time: n. the (.) during which something happens"
The use of a dictionary layout and the punctuation symbol for the word "period" combine to create a clever typographic visualization.

The bank of friendship cannot exist without deposits

93 Debra Salvucci,
"The bank of friendship cannot exist without deposits"

By the simple fashioning of a dollar sign from the letter "s," we see new life in an otherwise ordinary statement.

THE QUOTE POSTER

94 April Wong,
"I'm in search of myself have you seen me anywhere?"
The introduction of the magnifying glass becomes a key element in the visualization of this quandary.

Our Time Is A Very Shadow That Passeth Away.

WISDOM OF SOLOMON 2:5

96 Rosemarie O'Brien,
"In modern wedlock too many misplace the key"
Strong, bold typography, artfully placed, utilize the symbols of a lock and key to create the subtle emphasis.

95 Elizabeth DiFranza,
"Our time is a very shadow that passeth away"
A handsome rendering of a dramatic statement. The student uses shades of grey to achieve the fading effect, enhancing the visual play on the words and meaning.

THE QUOTE POSTER

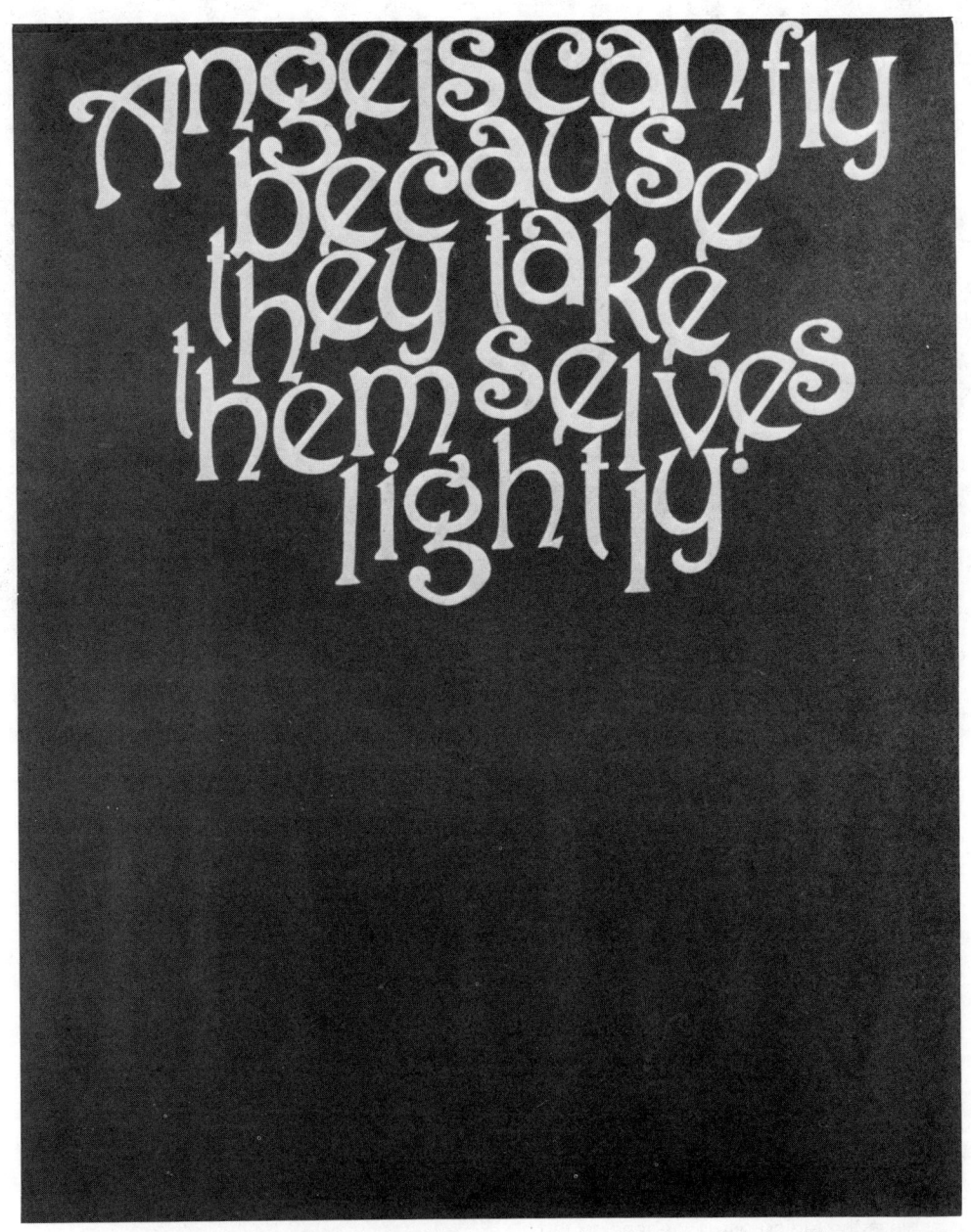

> Angels can fly because they take themselves lightly.

97　Carolina Marquez-Sterling, "Angels can fly because they take themselves lightly"
The whimsical type style and grouping of the words create the cloudlike appearance which is the key element in the visual meaning of the phrase.

nine
THE VEGETABLE POSTER

beets

Beets are an ancient vegetable, though the Greeks and Romans grew them for their leaves and not their roots. The succulent roots can be baked, pickled or boiled into a european soup called Borscht.

THE VEGETABLE POSTER

As we said in the previous chapter, a poster's chief function is to bring information to the attention of the public. This information usually incorporates favorable aspects of products and services or announces upcoming events. Another important role of the modern poster involves education. Such a poster is usually a mixture of aesthetic and educational elements designed as a teaching unit. I have seen these posters displayed in classrooms, doing the twofold job of decoration and positive reinforcement for various subjects and ideas. In these posters we can see information and image areas working together in a good relationship of form and function.

The problem to be solved in the assignment in this chapter is the discovery of an image that is universally comprehensible to the youngest of audiences, using an idea that has been translated into simple visual form. The poster needs to attract attention and hold a child or adult's interest while producing a clear and precise impression. In designing this poster, you should consider the three basic principles of design—*balance, emphasis, and unity.*

First we must attract our viewer's attention. In order to accomplish this, all the elements in a design should be arranged to bring about harmony and *balance*. This will ensure a viewer's immediate and favorable reaction. The second principle is *emphasis*. The focal point, or dominant element in the design, brings the viewer into the composition. Other elements then present themselves in a logical order (one of descending importance).

Unity, the third design principle, involves the planning and producing of a poster design (or

THE VEGETABLE POSTER

any design) as a unit. All the participating elements work together to form a single idea or theme. In composition, the most basic two-dimensional organization is known as the *figure/ ground* relationship. The viewer's attention is directed to the figure, or the central image area; the ground/background is equally important in the formulation of the viewer's perception of the design. Both the figure and background areas have distinct shapes and are usually perceived as positive and negative spaces (see figure 98).

Choose a vegetable you think would make good subject matter for a poster. Go to your supermarket and buy the vegetable to use as a model. First, draw pencil studies of the vegetable. Try to extract its unique characteristics until you have a pictorial description. Second, draw horizontal and vertical 1 x 2" boxes on your sketch paper, and begin thinking out possible arrangements for your image in different compositional formats. Test out ideas and concepts that might be related to the vegetable. For example, look at figure 99. We see a husk of corn with its kernels "popping" out and forming the word "corn." This is a clever idea, for very young people may not as yet have made the connection between corn on the cob and popcorn.

Look closely at the posters which illustrate this chapter. There would seem to be two approaches to this particular assignment. One is a relatively informal, pictorial approach illustrating the vegetable with a corresponding food or related surrounding; the second is a more formal, structural approach incorporating the vegetable in a strong compositional space where negative shape plays an important role.

THE VEGETABLE POSTER

98 Figure/ground variations. (a) simple ground; (b) figure over ground; (c) figure within ground; (d) ground as surface; (e) ground as space; (f) ground becomes figure.

THE VEGETABLE POSTER

The material for creating the final comp will be cut paper. When using cut paper to model your visual areas, keep in mind that you will need to abstract the shadow and highlight elements in order to create more of a three-dimensional illusion. To do this you will need a "blueprint." Draw your vegetable and detail the highlight and shadow areas. Break down these areas into distinct shapes. Choose your paper colors from Pantone® or Color-Aid paper swatchbooks. Make sure you choose colors with corresponding tints and shades. A *tint* is made from a color by mixing white into it. A *shade* is made from a color by mixing the color's complementary color into it. In color mixing with paints, for example, to achieve a lighter or "pinker" color from a particular red, you would mix white in with the red, and continue to mix more white until you have the "tint" of red you desire. To achieve a darker color from a particular red, you would mix green (red's complement on the color wheel) in with the red until you have the desired "shade." In fashioning a beet, you will need a tint of your color for the beet's highlight, and a darker shade of the color for the beet's shadow areas. By modeling your vegetable in this manner you will produce a three-dimensional effect rather than a flat shape cut from only one piece of paper. Study the student illustrations here to see how each one handled this shape illusion.

Reread Chapter 8 for details on working with cut paper and rubber cement. Always remember to use sharp X-acto® knife blades to cut these specialized papers. This will minimize white frayed edges. The size of the poster can be either 15 x 20" or 20 x 30", in a horizontal or vertical format.

THE VEGETABLE POSTER ASSIGNMENT

Design a poster using a vegetable as your subject matter.

Specifications

Copy: Name of the vegetable in a well-chosen or well-designed typestyle. Four or five sentences of body copy written to illustrate information about the vegetable.

Size: 15 x 20" or 20 x 30", horizontal or vertical.

Media: cut paper; no color restriction.

Materials needed

1. Tracing paper for sketches
2. Pencils for sketching
3. Color-Aid and/or Pantone® art papers
4. X-acto® knife and extra blades
5. Type book
6. Rubber cement and pick-up
7. 15 x 20" or 20 x 30" illustration board
8. The vegetable to be used as a model

Reference

American Institute of Graphic Arts. *AIGA Graphic Design USA 1: Annual of the American Institute of Graphic Arts.* New York: Watson-Guptill Publications, 1980.

American Institute of Graphic Arts. *AIGA Graphic Design USA 2: Annual of the American Institute of Graphic Arts.* New York: Watson-Guptill Publications, 1981.

American Institute of Graphic Arts. *AIGA Graphic Design USA 3: Annual of the American Institute of Graphic Arts.* New York: Watson-Guptill Publications, 1982.

Communication Arts Magazine. Palo Alto, California, published bimonthly.

Farland, Evelyn and Leo. *Posters By Painters.* New York: Harry N. Abrams, Inc., 1978.

Glaser, Milton. *The Milton Glaser Poster Book.* New York: Harmony Books, 1977.

Goines, David Lance. *The David Lance Goines Poster Book.* New York: Harmony Books, 1978.

Graphis Magazine. Switzerland, published bimonthly.

Graphis Posters. New York: Hastings House, published annually.

Hurlburt, Allen. *The Design Concept.* New York: Watson-Guptill Publications, 1981.

Karo, Jerzy. *Graphic Design: Problems, Methods, and Solutions.* New York: Van Nostrand Reinhold, 1975.

Rand, Paul. *Thoughts on Design.* New York and London: Van Nostrand Reinhold/Studio Vista, 1970.

THE VEGETABLE POSTER

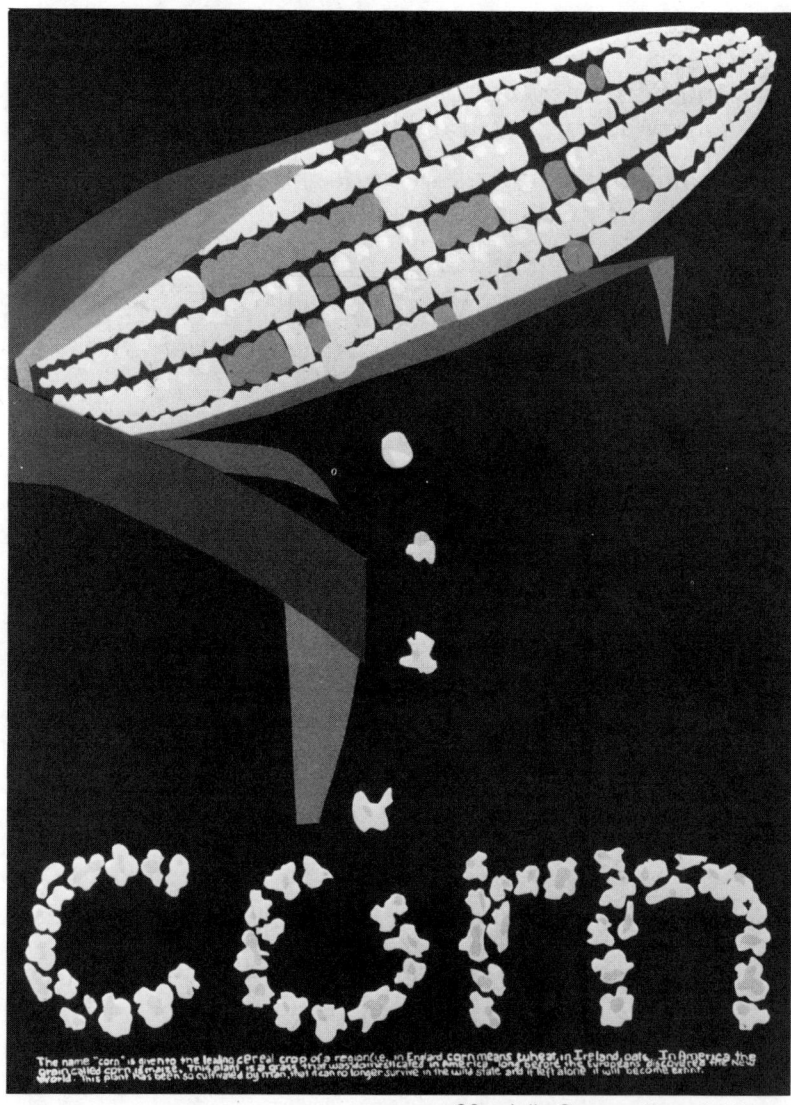

99 Julia Stearns Zaccai, "Corn"
Especially informative for very young audiences who may not be aware of the origins of popcorn, we see kernels of corn "popping out" from the husk to form the word "corn." The earthy colors of green, yellow, and white combine to make this poster a clever standout.

100 Deborah Chandler, "Brussels Sprouts" The floating vegetables create a feeling of suspended animation. Look to the fork in this design for an accurate account of the vegetable's size. The sensitivity in selecting the right grey background and the tints of earthy green to model the vegetables compliments the well composed compositional structure.
©1981 by Deborah Chandler

Oh the hidden talents of this versatile squash! Sliced, diced, fried, baked, broiled or steamed, zucchini tastes great!

ZUCCHINI

THE VEGETABLE POSTER

102 Rosemarie O'Brien, "Eggplant"
"Essence of Eggplant" is what I would name this poster. An excellent example of a figure/ground relationship where the positive and negative areas participate equally in the formulation of compositional structure. Simple styling of the lowercase letters reinforces the minimalist impression.

101 Nancy Pettibone, "Zucchini"
A "down on the farm" wooden box, the zucchini rainbow against puffy white clouds, and a very blue sky combine to create this warm, earthy scene.

THE VEGETABLE POSTER

103 Debra Salvucci, "Onion"
A study of the cross section of an onion, with its unique network of subtle lines, forms the basis of this student's poster. Patterns formed by nature are good design inspirations. Remember, the exquisiteness of nature's forms never go out of fashion.

104 Judith L. Pearson, "Peas"
Wonderfully bulbous letterforms act as suitable companions to a playful cartoon illustration.

peas

the common, or garden pea, an annual vine, has two or more white flowers on the flower stalk; the fruits or peas, which come from these are more or less round in form and green in color.

105 Tom Szumowski, "Beets"
Since he is primarily interested in illustration, this student's first thought was to create a pictorial scene involving his vegetable and its preparation in a food. This poster is a very appealing study involving good use of compositional space in creating its three-dimensional effect.

THE VEGETABLE POSTER

106 Maria Robba, "Artichoke"
This poster compliments the artichoke's unique characteristic of peeling layers to expose a "heart," the most succulent part of the vegetable. Shades of rich green and yellow are successfully modeled to form the artichoke. Background purples complete the picture.

THE VEGETABLE POSTER

107 Michele Cormier Biondo, "Eggplant"
Another equally successful interpretation of an eggplant, utilizing a friendly approach. The letterforms are well chosen and coordinate with the bulbous imagery. The vegetable has been modeled with shades of red violet.

108 Maria Sun, "Turk's Turban"
A dramatic presentation of these natural forms in a strong compositional base. Fine detail in the rendering combined with imaginative use of the body copy space make this study aesthetically beautiful. A black background adds drama as a contrast to the orange, green, and white forms.

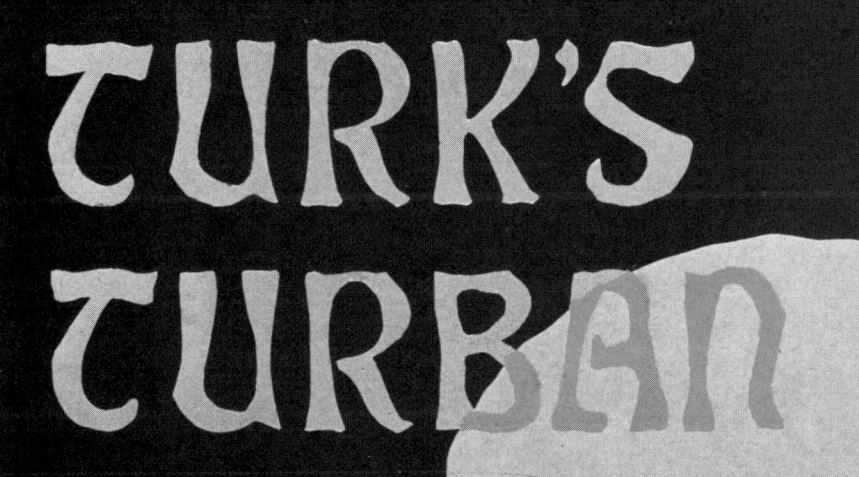

TURK'S TURBAN

...a squash which is so named because its shape resembles the headress worn by Turkish nomads. It is a winter variety with a hard outer skin and needs a long growing season. It can be stored for long periods for later eating in fall and winter. The distinctive bizarre markings make the Turk's Turban highly ornamental for Thanksgiving and Halloween.

Pepper

The pepper is a native of the New World tropics, but is also grown in warmer regions of the earth. Pepper plants are shrubby with oval leaves and white flowers that ripen into the many seeded, thick walled pepper.

THE VEGETABLE POSTER

110 David P. White, "Broccoli"
A great forest of broccoli forges to the foreground from the lower left-hand corner to fill three-quarters of the picture plane. The remaining one quarter of space forms an interesting negative shape. Again we see excellent modeling of the vegetable, utilizing shades and tints of green. The background color is a sea green (green with a blue cast).

109 Ramune Jauniskis, "Pepper"
There have been a number of "pepper" posters designed for this assignment through the years. I like this one in particular because of its good modeling detail and bold use of compositional spaces. The green forms are brought forth by the bright yellow ochre background.

CARROT

THE CARROT is an EDIBLE ROOT THAT's usually GROWN in PATCHES and sometimes EATEN in HOLES.

TOMATOES

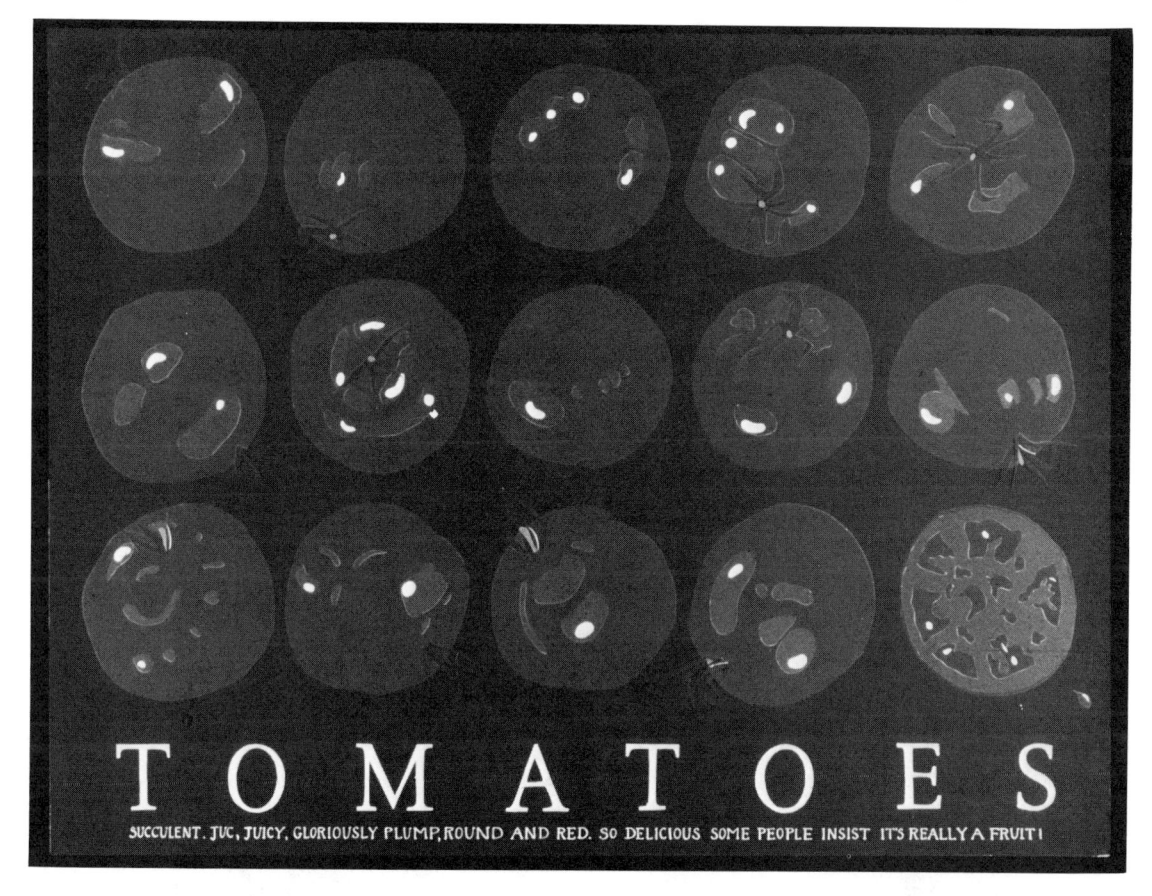

SUCCULENT. JUC, JUICY, GLORIOUSLY PLUMP, ROUND AND RED. SO DELICIOUS SOME PEOPLE INSIST IT'S REALLY A FRUIT!

112 Plum Gerstein, "Tomatoes"
A striking combination of rich royal blue and bright red-orange combine to lend strength to this attractive design based on image repetition. The lifelike tomatoes are particularly well drawn, modeled with shadow and highlight shapes. Good typography supports but does not detract from the initial imagery.

111 Luis-Miguel Muelle, "Carrot"
This humorous cartoon illustration of a rabbit in his home below the carrot patch supports the playful association begun with Peter Rabbit and Bugs Bunny. Earthy colors with unusual, well-designed typography add to the conceptually strong compositional base.

ten
THE COUNTRY POSTER

The main emphasis of discussion in each assignment throughout this book has been the development of a *design concept*. By now you have discovered that such is not an easy feat. **The design concept is an invisible thread weaving the entire composition together while creating a cohesive hierarchy of all the participating visual elements.** At the risk of repetition, I think it is important to review the design process step-by-step:

1. Listen attentively to (or read carefully) the problem as stated. Each problem contains a set of constraints inherent in its unique makeup.

2. Remember—each problem is represented in terms of visual imagery, and this imagery must be appropriate to the subject at hand.

3. Explore the range of visual images that come to mind by jotting down each one in the form of a thumbnail sketch. Resist the temptation to dwell on one particular idea which might prevent the flow of other ideas from surfacing.

4. If need be, review visual resource materials gathered from libraries, photographs, design magazines and annuals, and your own files to help stimulate the flow of ideas.

5. Before making the final selection from your sketch ideas, wait a few hours or overnight. Your sketches will often be seen in a new light when you review them with a fresh eye. Not all your ideas will seem as successful upon a second or third appraisal.

6. Realize the limitations of a thumbnail sketch, especially as you scale the sketch proportions up to the specified size. The strength of the concept and/or compositional space may suffer in the enlargement.

7. And finally, a solution selected and pre-

THE COUNTRY POSTER

sented by you should attempt to solve the proposed problem, not create others.

Remember—design is a decision-making process; a successful piece is born of many careful decisions at each juncture.

Think of a country you have read about or visited. In the past you will recall seeing symbols like the Eiffel Tower, Union Jack, or the Pyramids representing countries. These symbols evoke different sensations in each person. Your mind imagines each country, using colors, images, sounds, and perhaps smells to create a picture. In this assignment you will design a poster on a country of your choice. This will involve a graphic interpretation exploring your visual perception. Try to steer clear of established symbols like the ones mentioned above. Go after newer representations. If a particular symbol or figure is important in your concept, present it in a unique way, thus individualizing the image. The library is an important resource for locating picture books on countries, and most libraries have the added bonus of picture files to look through. Magazines like *National Geographic* and *Geo* provide excellent sources for international photographs, sometimes depicting unusual scenes not often shown in the picture books.

The only copy to appear on your poster is the name of the country. The typography should be closely woven into the concept or imagery and not set apart as a separate element. One approach can involve the typography as the foundation of the image (see figure 114). It is best to promote only one image or idea in your composition. For example, look at figure 113 on Haiti, a small island in the Caribbean Ocean. The student singled out the importance of straw as a useful everyday part of Haitian life by presenting the portrait of a native islander and her market basket with the island's name woven into its design. The warm colors of orange, red, yellow, and brown blend to produce the overall sensation of a hot and tropical place.

Statements on prevalent political situations are also encouraged as they are relevant expressions of a country's personality. The poster on Iran (figure 115) was designed in the midst of their civil war to overthrow the Shah's government. It is a masterfully simple statement of political tyranny.

The size of your poster is to be 15 x 20" or 20 x 30", either vertical or horizontal. Pantone® and Color-Aid papers have a wide range of hues, tints, and shades available, so we will use cut paper as a building material. I also find that using cut paper offers more of a challenge when illustrating figures as three-dimensional objects because you must carefully plan your highlight and shadow areas as shapes and forms.

THE COUNTRY POSTER ASSIGNMENT

Choose a country anywhere in the world (perhaps one you have never visited, or are not familiar with). Research the country through pictures in order to graphically interpret the *feeling, design, and color* of that country in visual form.

The only copy to appear on the poster is the name of the country woven into the imagery or composition.

Specifications

Copy: name of country.

Size: 15 x 20" or 20 x 30", horizontal or vertical.

THE COUNTRY POSTER

Media: cut paper; no color restriction.

Materials needed

1. Tracing paper for sketches
2. Pencils for sketching
3. Color-Aid and/or Pantone® art papers
4. X-acto® knife and extra blades
5. Type book
6. Rubber cement and pick-up
7. 15 x 20" or 20 x 30" illustration board
8. Picture reference material

Reference

American Institute of Graphic Arts. *AIGA Graphic Design USA 1: Annual of the American Institute of Graphic Arts.* New York: Watson-Guptill Publications, 1980.

American Institute of Graphic Arts. *AIGA Graphic Design USA 2: Annual of the American Institute of Graphic Arts.* New York: Watson-Guptill Publications, 1981.

American Institute of Graphic Arts. *AIGA Graphic Design USA 3: Annual of the American Institute of Graphic Arts.* New York: Watson-Guptill Publications, 1982.

Communication Arts Magazine. Palo Alto, California, published bimonthly.

Farland, Evelyn and Leo. *Posters By Painters.* New York: Harry N. Abrams, Inc., 1978.

Geo Magazine. Los Angeles: Knapp Communications Corporation, published monthly.

Glaser, Milton. *The Milton Glaser Poster Book.* New York: Harmony Books, 1977.

Goines, David Lance. *The David Lance Goines Poster Book.* New York: Harmony Books, 1978.

Graphis Magazine. Switzerland, published bimonthly.

Graphis Posters. New York: Hastings House, published annually.

Hurlburt, Allen. *The Design Concept.* New York: Watson-Guptill Publications, 1981.

Karo, Jerzy. *Graphic Design: Problems, Methods, and Solutions.* New York: Van Nostrand Reinhold, 1975.

National Geographic Magazine. Washington, D.C.: The National Geographic Society, published monthly.

Rand, Paul. *Thoughts on Design.* New York and London: Van Nostrand Reinhold/Studio Vista, 1970.

Statements on prevalent political situations are encouraged as relevant expressions of a country's current personality. Posters 115, 116, and 117 are good examples of this design direction.

113 Judith Anthony, "Haiti"
A portrait of a Haitian woman with her market basket. The typography becomes a skillfully woven basket design and the rich warm colors of orange, yellow, red, and brown blend to symbolize the climate and locale. The student selected this portrait from a photographic essay on Haiti published in *National Geographic* magazine.

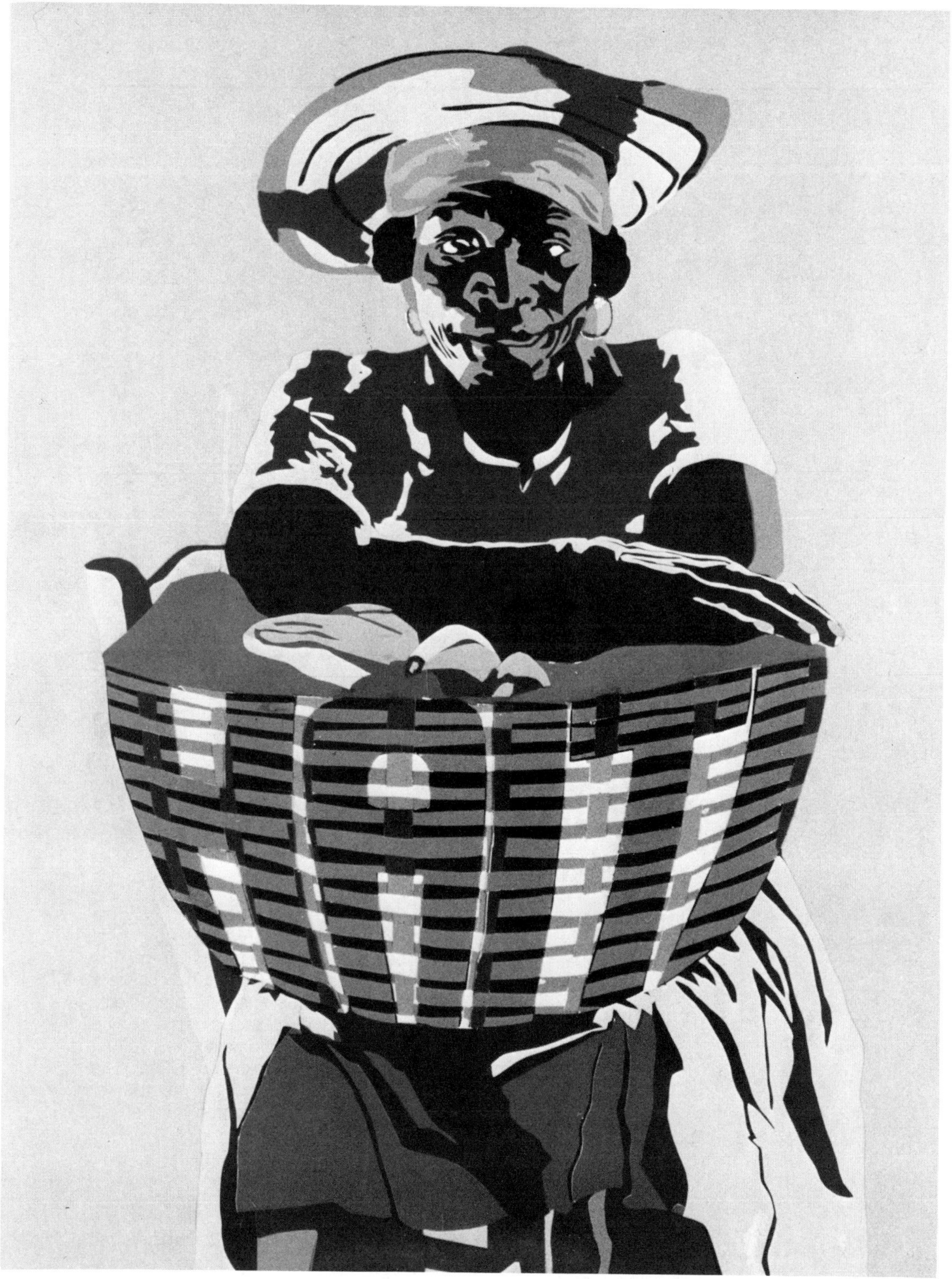

THE COUNTRY POSTER

114 Tullie Warshauer, "Egypt"
A good example of figurative typographic design as the concept foundation. The student fashioned the letterforms into a pyramid and carefully placed other objects in the background for added depth. Notice that where the sun would strike the pyramid on its left side, the colors are lighter. The right side is in shadow and therefore darker to create the three-dimensional effect.

115 James Edwards, "Iran"
Designed during the period of Iran's civil war which ended the Shah's regime, this poster is a masterfully simple political statement.

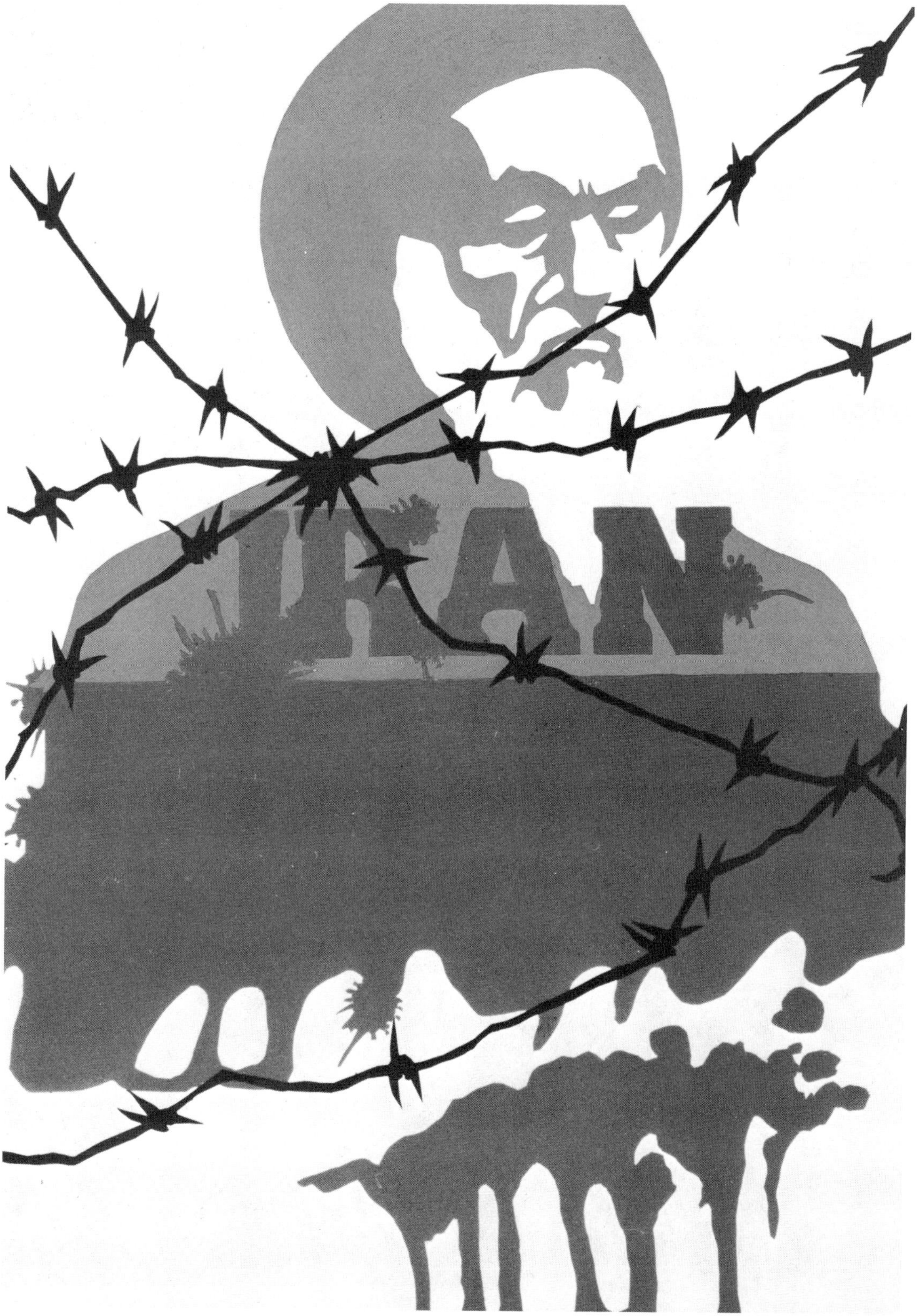
IRAN

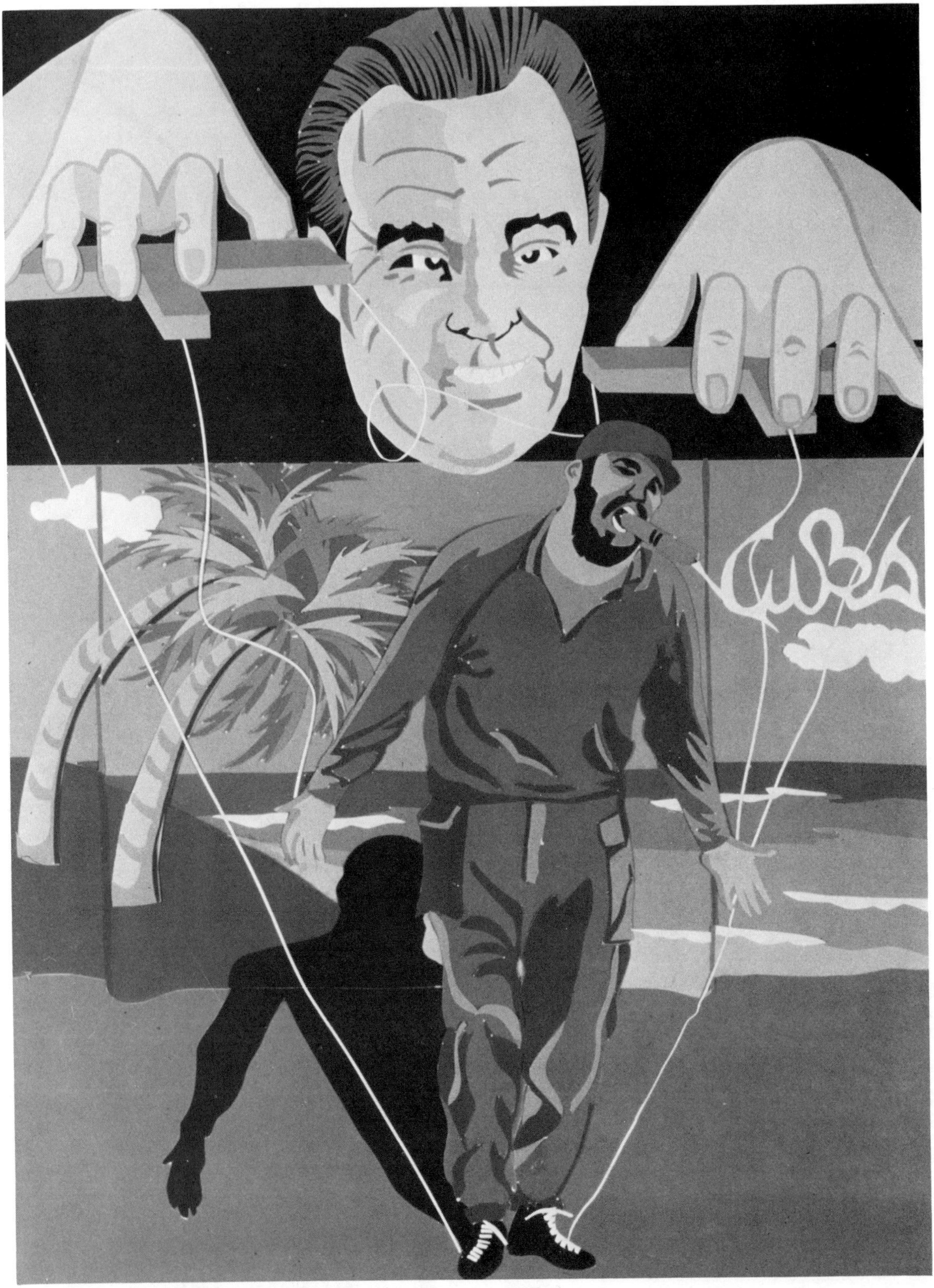

117 Philip Reavis, Jr., "South Africa"
A dramatically powerful typographic demonstration of apartheid in the Republic of South Africa. The student employed a symbolic color scheme, using gold for the shape of the country, white letters for "South," black letters for "Africa," and red for the dripping blood illustration.

116 Carolina Marquez-Sterling, "Cuba"
Motivated by her Cuban heritage, this student was concerned with making a firm statement on a recent mass exodus of Cuban refugees searching for freedom. She comments, "To introduce an identifiable historical motive, I used the colors red and black, which were the colors of [Castro's] July 26 movement in the 1950s."

118 Ramune Jauniskis, "China" The black outline in this poster is cut from one sheet of paper. I asked Ramune to comment on her subject and technique. "I had been taking an Asian Art course at the time the assignment was given and I asked my instructor for suggestions about China. One of her suggestions was to look into Chinese paper cuts. As the assignment was to be done in cut paper, I thought the paper cuts idea would be a good choice. I wanted to make the poster look like China yet not have the conventional Oriental look. In doing the poster, I tried to make the paper cut exactly as the Chinese made them—by cutting the black outline from one piece of paper and then placing the colored areas underneath. I went through the process in the same manner as the Chinese and have gained a real understanding of the time and patience that goes into this art."

119   Maryann Cocca, "Italy"
Influenced by her Italian heritage, Maryann decided to do her poster on that country. "In my house it is always 'eat, eat.' Food is an important part of Italian festivities and customs. I felt [that] of all foods, spaghetti expressed Italy the best. In my sketches I composed the illustration several ways: without the bowl; just the fork of spaghetti; with a hand holding the fork; with the entire bowl and checkered tablecloth, etc. I decided to concentrate on the main idea, the spaghetti, and incorporated the word "Italy" in the spaghetti itself. This was not only an illustrator's approach to this problem but also a humorous statement about Italy and its connection with food."

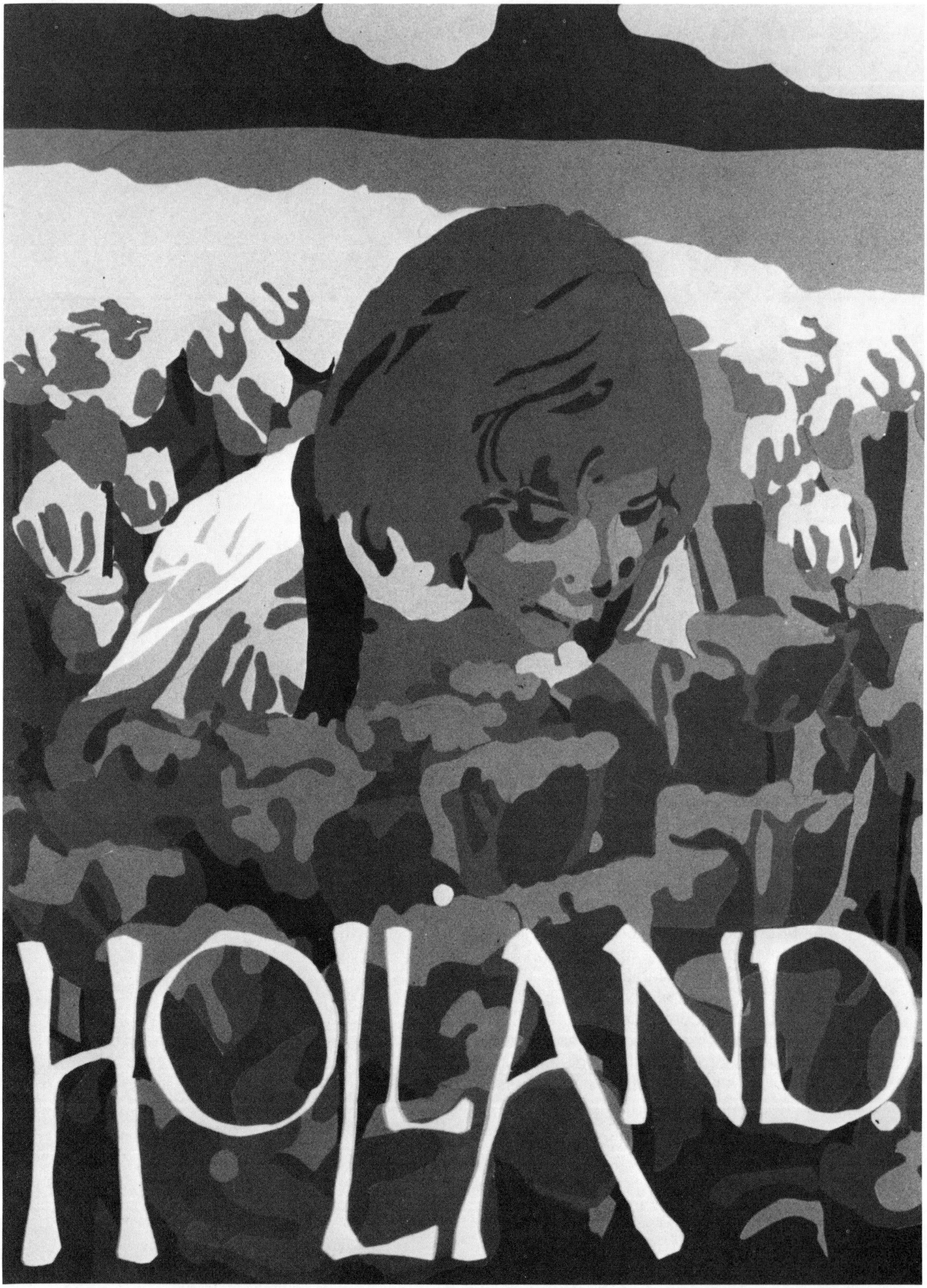
HOLLAND.

121 Lorraine Silvestri, "Mexico"
A strong design motif dominates the compositional structure. Note how the typography is firmly woven into the fabric of the motif. Together with the chromatic combination of orange, pink, red, and brown, we can sense the hot and dusty landscape of Mexico.

120 Jeanne Loerch Neverisky, "Holland"
Research is extremely important in assisting with the decision-making process. I asked Jeanne to comment on her experience in creating this exquisite piece of design. "The first thing I did was to go to the library and browse through books on the countries I was interested in. I did this to get a feel for the 'flavor' of each country and to note some of their visual characteristics. I decided on Holland, as I had lived there for three years. Because much of Holland is actually quaint, the motifs in my roughs look trite—wooden shoes, tulips, windmills, cheese—anyone could have come up with these images. I was disappointed with my tourist-y roughs, but remembered a certain photograph our family had taken in Holland and I studied it. The picture was a more of a personal look than any design I had tried or any travel photo. I liked the straightforwardness and honesty of the nonposed figure with the flowers and wanted my poster to look like you had just turned around and caught a glimpse of this scene. I worked with the picture, simplified the image to translate it into flat colors. The typography evolved by writing and rewriting 'Holland,' trying to fit the word into the space. For me the letterforms are reminiscent of the tall, narrow, decorative buildings you could see in Amsterdam and the country's folk art. This poster incorporates twenty-odd colors of Color-Aid paper and it took many hours to complete, from making the pattern to cutting and pasting down the pieces. I felt it was the only way to accomplish what I wanted to do."

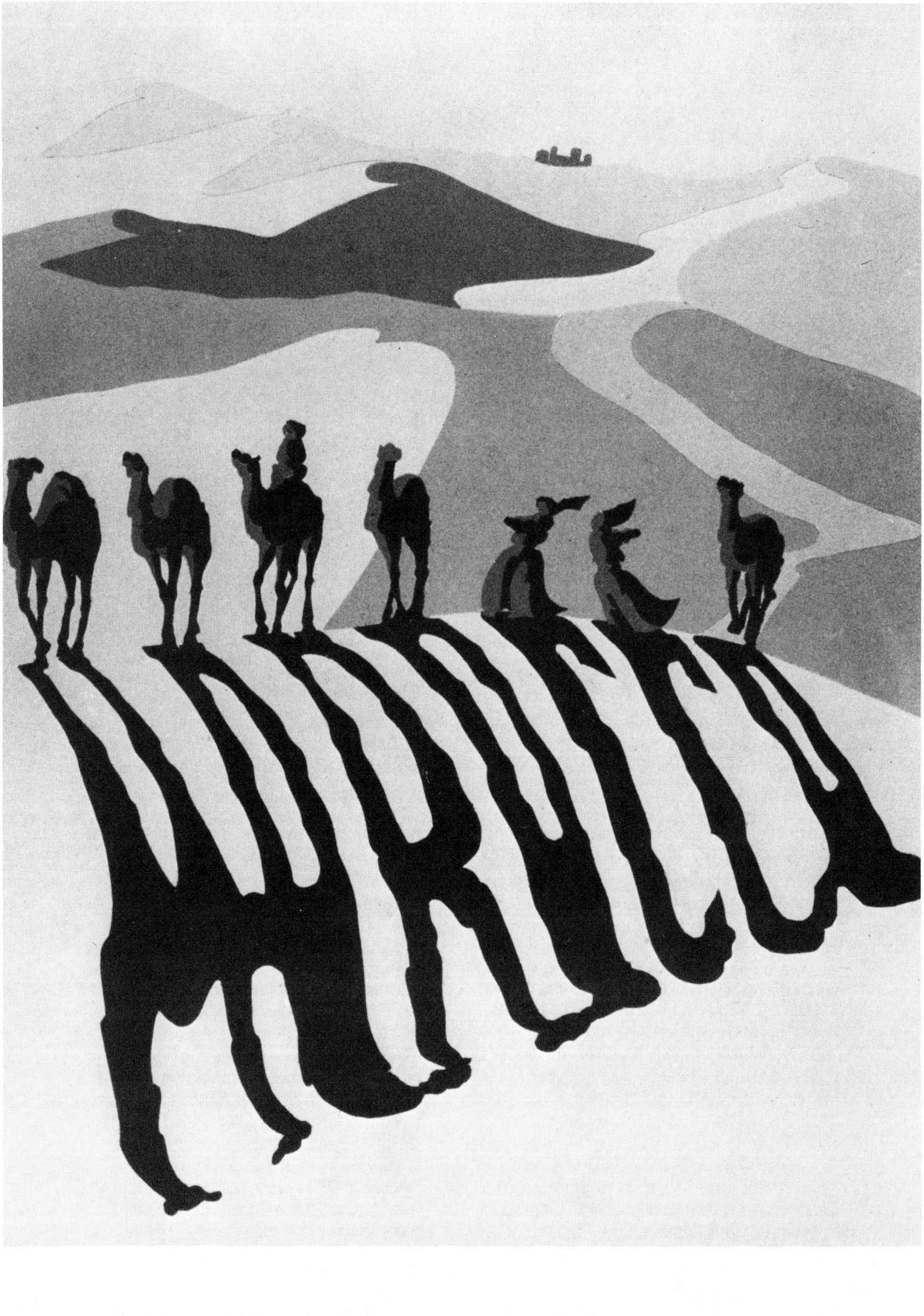

123 Deborah Chandler, "Norway"
I find this simple and straightforward poster an excellent example of typographic illustration.
©1981 by Deborah Chandler

122 Carol Greger, "Morocco"
Concerned with creating a strong piece of design for her portfolio, this student spent many hours drawing and redrawing camels. "It took a while to figure out [if a camel could] cast a C-shaped shadow. After I figured out how to make all the letters and put the camels together in a line, I began to work on what the shadow shapes could possibly look like. I did sketches working on the angles of letters, how long the shadows were going to be, and how big the horizon line would be in comparison to everything else. I also did many color roughs, as I was very unsure of the colors I wanted to use. I think I bought at least ten sheets of Pantone® paper and changed a lot of the background shapes while working on the actual finished piece. I did this because the actual color changed some of the balances I had previously worked out." There is an extraordinary sense of color design demonstrated in this poster. Maroon, pinks, light blues, blue, and red violet make up the desert environment.

bibliography

American Institute of Graphic Arts. *AIGA Graphic Design USA 1: Annual of the American Institute of Graphic Arts.* New York: Watson-Guptill Publications, 1980.

_____.*AIGA Graphic Design USA 2: Annual of the American Institute of Graphic Arts.* New York: Watson-Guptill Publications, 1981.

_____.*AIGA Graphic Design USA 3: Annual of the American Institute of Graphic Arts.* New York: Watson-Guptill Publications, 1982.

_____.*Symbol Signs.* New York: Hastings House, 1981.

Berryman, Gregg. *Notes on Graphic Design and Visual Communication.* Los Angeles: William Kaufmann, Inc., 1979.

Bevlin, Marjorie Elliott. *Design Through Discovery.* New York: Holt, Rinehart and Winston, Inc., 1977.

Burns, Aaron. *Typography.* New York: Reinhold Publishing Company, 1961.

Craig, James. *Designing with Type.* New York: Watson-Guptill Publications, 1971.

de Sausmarez, Maurice. *Basic Design: The Dynamics of Visual Form.* London and New York: Studio Vista/Van Nostrand Reinhold, 1964.

Donahue, Bud. *The Language of Layout.* Englewood Cliffs, N.J.: Prentice-Hall, Inc., 1978.

Dreyfuss, Henry. *Symbol Sourcebook.* New York: McGraw-Hill Book Company, 1972.

Dürer, Albrecht. *Of The Just Shaping of Letters.* New York: Dover Publications, 1965.

Farland, Evelyn and Leo. *Posters By Painters.* New York: Harry N. Abrams, Inc., 1978.

Felde, Nathan, and Julius Friedman. *Public Works*. Louisville, Kentucky: Hawley, Cooke and Orr, Publishers, 1980.

Gates, David. *Type*. New York: Watson-Guptill Publications, 1973.

Gill, Bob. *Forget All The Rules You Ever Learned about Graphic Design*. New York: Watson-Guptill Publications, 1981.

Glaser, Milton. *The Milton Glaser Poster Book*. New York: Harmony Books, 1977.

Goines, David Lance. *The David Lance Goines Poster Book*. New York: Harmony Books, 1978.

Goodchild, Jon, and Bill Henkin. *By Design: A Graphics Sourcebook of Materials, Equipment and Services*. New York: Quick Fox, 1980.

Graphis Posters. New York: Hastings House, published annually.

Haley, Allan. *Phototypography*. New York: Charles Scribner's Sons, 1980.

Hofmann, Armin. *Graphic Design Manual*. New York: Van Nostrand Reinhold, 1965.

Hurlburt, Allen. *The Design Concept*. New York: Watson-Guptill Publications, 1981.

Hurlburt, Allen. *The Grid*. New York: Van Nostrand Reinhold, 1978.

Karo, Jerzy. *Graphic Design: Problems, Methods, and Solutions*. New York: Van Nostrand Reinhold, 1975.

Koberg, Don, and Jim Bagnall. *The Universal Traveler*. Los Angeles: William Kaufmann, Inc., 1972.

BIBLIOGRAPHY

Kuwayama, Yasaburo. *Trademarks & Symbols.* New York: Van Nostrand Reinhold, 1973.

Lauer, David A. *Design Basics.* New York: Holt, Rinehart and Winston, 1979.

List, Vera, and Herbert Kupferberg. *Lincoln Center Posters.* New York: Harry N. Abrams, Inc., 1980.

Longyear, William. *Type and Lettering.* New York: Watson-Guptill Publications, 1966.

Maier, Manfred. *Basic Principles of Design.* New York: Van Nostrand Reinhold, 1980.

McKim, Robert H. *Experiences in Visual Thinking.* Monterey, California: Brooks/Cole Publishing Company, 1972.

Modley, Rudolf. *Handbook of Pictorial Symbols.* New York: Dover Publications, 1976.

Oskerse, Thomas. *Visible Language and Graphic Design Education.* Bulletin of the Rhode Island School of Design, March 1980.

Rand, Paul. *Thoughts on Design.* London and New York: Studio Vista/Van Nostrand Reinhold, 1970.

Rosen, Ben. *Type and Typography.* New York: Van Nostrand Reinhold, 1963.

Ruder, Emil. *Typography.* New York: Hastings House, 1967.

Scott, Robert Gilliam. *Design Fundamentals.* New York: McGraw-Hill Book Company, 1951.

Taylor, Richard. *A Basic Course in Graphic Design.* London and New York: Studio Vista/Van Nostrand Reinhold, 1965.

Typography 1: The Annual of the Type Directors Club. New York: Watson-Guptill Publications, 1980.

Typography 2: The Annual of the Type Directors Club. New York: Watson-Guptill Publications, 1981.

Typography 3: The Annual of the Type Directors Club. New York: Watson-Guptill Publications, 1982.

U&lc, The International Journal of Typographics. New York: International Typeface Corporation, published quarterly.

Wildbur, Peter. *International Trademark Design.* New York: Van Nostrand Reinhold, 1979.

Wong, Wucius. *Principles of Two-Dimensional Design.* New York: Van Nostrand Reinhold, 1972.

index

ascender, 24, 25

balance, 104
baseline (of type), 24, 25
brushes, 4–5

color, 107
Color-Aid paper, 6
compass, 4
composition, defined, 92
counter (of type), 24, 25
country poster assignment, 125–42
   student work, 131–42

descender, 24, 25
designers gouache, 6
drafting tape, 5
drawing board, 4

emphasis, 104
erasers, 5

figure/ground relationship, 105, 106, 113
form, 10, 16

illustration board, 6
illustrative typography, 51–60
ink, 4, 5

Letraset Catalog, 6
letterform collage assignment, 9–22
   student work, 15, 17–22
letterform progression assignment, 37–50
   student work, 39–41, 46–50
letters, relationship of (see relationship of letters assignment)
lowercase letters, 24, 25

mail order supplies, 7–8
masking tape, 5
materials and tools, 3–8
   for country poster assignment, 129
   for letterform collage assignment, 16
   for letterform progression assignment, 44
   for quote poster assignment, 94
   for relationship of letters assignment, 27–28
   for self-promotion typography assignment, 74–75
   for simple tool assignment, 83
   for vegetable poster assignment, 107, 108
   for word action progression assignment, 55
   for word play typography assignment, 65
mat knife, 5, 6
movement, 10–11, 16, 17

Pantone® Color Paper, 6
papers, 6, 107
parallel-rule drawing board, 4
pencils, 5
pens, 4, 5
pictograph, 38, 43
posters:
   country, 125–42
   quote, 91–102
   vegetable, 103–24

quote poster assignment, 91–102
   student work, 95–102

rapidographs, 4
relationship of letters assignment, 23–36
   student work, 29–36
rhythm, 38
rubber cement, 5, 6
rubber cement pick-up, 5, 7
rubber cement solvent and dispenser, 5, 7
rulers, 4
ruling pen set, 4

sans serif, 24, 25
self-promotion typography assignment, 71–80
   student work, 73, 76–80
serif, 24, 25
shade, 107
simple tool assignment, 81–90
   student work, 84–90
stem (of type), 24, 25

technical fountain pens, 4, 5
texture, 11, 16
thumbnail sketch, 43, 126
tint, 107
tools (see materials and tools)
tracing paper, 6

triangles, 4
T-square, 3
type book, 6–7

unity, 104
uppercase letters, 24, 25
utility knife, 5, 6

vegetable poster assignment, 103–24
  student work, 110–24
visual progression, 38, 52

word action progression assignment, 51–60
  student work, 56–60
word play typography assignment, 61–70
  student work, 63–64, 67–70

X-acto® knife, 5, 6, 107
x-height, 24, 25